TWIN VOLCANIC CONES GUARDING ST. LUCIA

SOOTY TERNS ON AVES ISLAND'S BEACH

EERIE GALLERY OF NATURAL SCULPTURE IN A JAMAICA CAVE

A BUSY CORAL REEF OFF BONAIRE

SUNSET OVER THE COAST AT ST. JOHN, VIRGIN ISLANDS

A WAVE-WASHED LIMESTONE BLUFF ON DOMINICA

ELKHORN CORALS AT LOW TIDE ON BONAIRE

TIME
LIFE
BOOKS

HUMAN BEHAVIOR
THE ART OF SEWING
THE OLD WEST
THE EMERGENCE OF MAN
THE AMERICAN WILDERNESS
THE TIME-LIFE ENCYCLOPEDIA OF GARDENING
LIFE LIBRARY OF PHOTOGRAPHY
THIS FABULOUS CENTURY
FOODS OF THE WORLD
TIME-LIFE LIBRARY OF AMERICA
TIME-LIFE LIBRARY OF ART
GREAT AGES OF MAN
LIFE SCIENCE LIBRARY
THE LIFE HISTORY OF THE UNITED STATES
TIME READING PROGRAM
LIFE NATURE LIBRARY
LIFE WORLD LIBRARY
FAMILY LIBRARY:
   HOW THINGS WORK IN YOUR HOME
   THE TIME-LIFE BOOK OF THE FAMILY CAR
   THE TIME-LIFE FAMILY LEGAL GUIDE
   THE TIME-LIFE BOOK OF FAMILY FINANCE

CARIBBEAN ISLES

THE AMERICAN WILDERNESS/TIME-LIFE BOOKS/NEW YORK

BY PETER WOOD

AND THE EDITORS OF TIME-LIFE BOOKS

TIME-LIFE BOOKS

FOUNDER: Henry R. Luce 1898-1967

Editor in Chief: Hedley Donovan
Chairman of the Board: Andrew Heiskell
President: James R. Shepley
Group Vice President: Rhett Austell

Vice Chairman: Roy E. Larsen

MANAGING EDITOR: Jerry Korn
Assistant Managing Editors: Ezra Bowen,
David Maness, Martin Mann, A. B. C. Whipple
Planning Director: Oliver E. Allen
Art Director: Sheldon Cotler
Chief of Research: Beatrice T. Dobie
Director of Photography: Melvin L. Scott
Senior Text Editor: Diana Hirsh
Assistant Art Director: Arnold C. Holeywell
Assistant Chief of Research: Myra Mangan

PUBLISHER: Joan D. Manley
General Manager: John D. McSweeney
Business Manager: Nicholas J. C. Ingleton
Sales Director: Carl G. Jaeger
Promotion Director: Paul R. Stewart
Public Relations Director: Nicholas Benton

THE AMERICAN WILDERNESS
SERIES EDITOR: Robert Morton
Editorial Staff for *Caribbean Isles:*
Text Editors: Philip W. Payne,
Rosalind Stubenberg
Picture Editor: Jane D. Scholl
Designer: Charles Mikolaycak
Staff Writers: Sally Clark, Carol Clingan,
Alice Kantor, John von Hartz
Chief Researcher: Martha T. Goolrick
Researchers: Paula Arno, Muriel Clarke,
Villette Harris, Beatrice Hsia,
Trish Kiesewetter, Mary Carroll Marden,
Yvonne Wong, Editha Yango
Design Assistant: Vincent Lewis

Editorial Production
Production Editor: Douglas B. Graham
Assistant Production Editors: Gennaro C. Esposito,
Feliciano Madrid
Quality Director: Robert L. Young
Assistant Quality Director: James J. Cox
Copy Staff: Eleanore W. Karsten (chief),
Barbara Quarmby, Susan Tribich,
Florence Keith, Pearl Sverdlin
Picture Department: Dolores A. Littles,
Joan Lynch
Traffic: Carmen McLellan

Valuable assistance was given by the following
departments and individuals of Time Inc.:
Editorial Production, Norman Airey; Library,
Benjamin Lightman; Picture Collection,
Doris O'Neil; Photographic Laboratory,
George Karas; TIME-LIFE News Service,
Murray J. Gart.

The Author: An island dweller by birth and by choice, Peter Wood has never been far from the sea; he grew up in Manhattan, and lives on Block Island in the Atlantic Ocean at the eastern entrance to Long Island Sound. For this book he made four trips to the Caribbean, having sailed and snorkeled in its waters many times before. Formerly on the staff of TIME-LIFE BOOKS, Wood has written articles for *The New York Times Magazine, The New Yorker* and other publications.

The Cover: Coconut palms fringe a corner of sandy beach on the island of Tobago—a scene evocative of many another Caribbean shore. The tree's omnipresence is due in part to the impressive durability and buoyancy of its fruits. Protected by a thick husk, a coconut can stay in salt water for as long as four months and still retain the power to germinate. Thus, when a coconut happens to be washed into the sea, it may drift 1,000 miles or more before it is driven ashore on another island, where it takes root to help swell the palm population there.

Contents

A Green-clad Island Arc

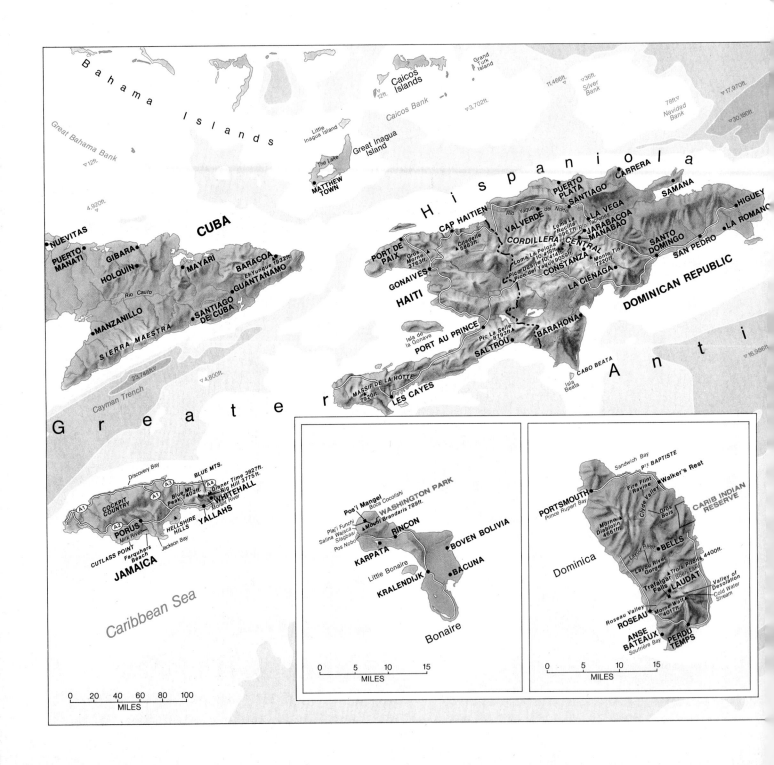

Bahama Islands

Great Bahama Bank
▽12ft.

Caicos Islands

Grand Turk Island

11,466ft.▽

▽36ft. Silver Bank

78ft.▽ Navidad Bank

▽17,970ft.

▽30,180ft.

Little Inagua Island

▽12ft.

Great Inagua Island

The Lake

MATTHEW TOWN

▽3,702ft.

CUBA

4,920ft. ▽

NUEVITAS

PUERTO MANATI

GIBARA

HOLQUIN

MAYARI

BARACOA El Yunque 1932ft.

Rio Cauto

MANZANILLO

SANTIAGO DE CUBA

GUANTANAMO

SIERRA MAESTRA

23,748ft.▽

▽4,800ft.

Cayman Trench

G r e a t e r

H i s p a n i o l a

CARRERA

PUERTO PLATA

SANTIAGO

SAMANA

CAP HAITIEN

Rio Yaque del Norte

VALVERDE

LA VEGA

HIGUEY

Loma La Rucilla 996.7ft. Rio Tablones

JARABACOA

MANABAO

LA ROMANA

Citadelle 583.3ft.

CORDILLERA CENTRAL

SANTO DOMINGO

PORT DE PAIX

Gros Morne 3763ft.

Loma La Pelona 10,416ft.

Pico Duarte 10,414ft. Pico del Yaque 905ft.

Monte Tina 7220ft.

CONSTANZA

SAN PEDRO

GONAIVES

LA CIENAGA

HAITI

DOMINICAN REPUBLIC

Isla de la Gonave

PORT AU PRINCE

Pic La Selle 8793ft.

SALTROU

BARAHONA

A n t i

▽16,986ft.

CABO BEATA

Isla Beata

MASSIF DE LA HOTTE 7920ft.

LES CAYES

Caribbean Sea

Jamaica (inset)

Discovery Bay

BLUE MTS.

Dinner Time 3827ft. Big Hill 3775ft.

A3

COCKPIT COUNTRY

A1

Blue Mt. Peak 402ft.

WHITEHALL

A1

Morant River

PORUS

HELLSHIRE HILLS

YALLAHS

A2

CUTLASS POINT

Farquhars Beach

Milk River

Jackson Bay

JAMAICA

Bonaire (inset)

Pos'i Mangel
Boca Cocolishi

WASHINGTON PARK

Plai'i Funchi Salina Waiaca Slagbaai

Pos Nobo

▲Mount Brandaris 789ft.

RINCON

BOVEN BOLIVIA

KARPATA

Little Bonaire

BACUNA

KRALENDIJK

Bonaire

0   5   10   15
MILES

Dominica (inset)

Sandwich Bay

P¹ᵉ BAPTISTE

Walker's Rest

Fire Flint Ravine

Clyde Valley

PORTSMOUTH
Prince Rupert Bay

Gros Bois

CARIB INDIAN RESERVE

Morne Diablotin 4661ft.

Layou River

BELLS

Layou River Gorge

Trois Pitons 4400ft.

Boeri Lake

Trafalgar Falls

LAUDAT

Valley of Desolation Cold Water Stream

Roseau Valley

Morne Watt 4017ft.

ROSEAU

ANSE BATEAUX

PERDU TEMPS

Soufriere Bay

Dominica

0   5   10   15
MILES

0   20   40   60   80   100
MILES

Embracing a warm and fecund sea, the islands of the Caribbean comprise two major groups, the Greater and Lesser Antilles. To the west lie Cuba, Jamaica, Hispaniola and Puerto Rico. Curving like a shepherd's crook to the east are the smaller islands —some of them, such as Aves off Dominica, mere pinpoints in the sea.

Despite centuries of colonization and yearly flocks of sun-seeking tourists, these islands still contain wild areas of dazzling diversity: 10,000-foot mountains, vine-choked rain forests, labyrinths of limestone caves and colorful coral reefs.

Inset on the area map below are large-scale views of two small islands that the author explored in detail. On all the maps, dark green stands for lowlands, yellow indicates hills and white denotes peaks. Blue lines trace rivers and streams, red lines enclose protected areas described in the book.

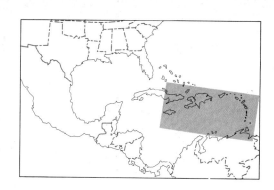

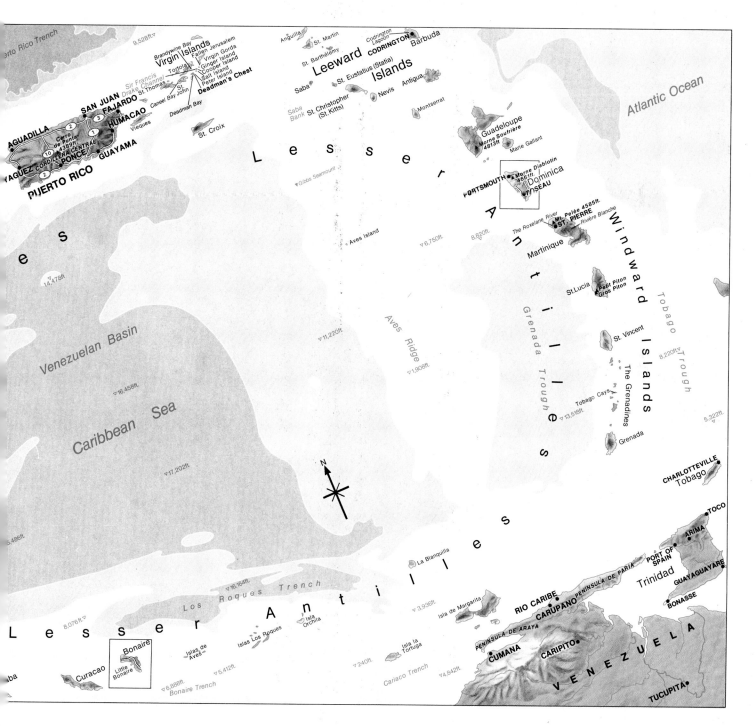

1/ A Glistening Archipelago

The enormous silent poem of color and light...
of sea and sky, of the woods and the peaks,
so far surpasses imagination as to paralyze it.

LAFCADIO HEARN/ *TWO YEARS IN THE FRENCH WEST INDIES*

Recalling Cuba, Christopher Columbus wrote that he had "never beheld so fair a thing; trees all along the river, beautiful and green and different from ours with flowers and fruits each according to their kind and little birds that sing very sweetly." Men reared under the sway of the chill and moody North Atlantic have always responded with such romantic flourishes to the charm of the Antilles, a radiant sea wall of mountains, volcanic peaks, rocks, cays, reefs and pinnacles that curls in a great arc around the northeast quadrant of the Caribbean (*map, pages 18-19*). This island barrier against the rough Atlantic sweeps from the western tip of Cuba 1,200 miles east to the Virgin Islands, south another 500 miles to the top of South America and then west another 500 along the coast of Venezuela—a chain of enchantment that captivates men's minds as surely and as firmly as it encircles the Caribbean Sea.

Four centuries after Columbus, in the summer of 1887, the American writer and world traveler Lafcadio Hearn took ship for the islands and found the Antilles as beguiling as ever. "You who know only the North do not know color, do not know light," he scribbled in his diary, in which abounds the refrain, "always the warm wind blowing." Later he described one of the islands as it appeared from the deck of the steam sailer on which he was a passenger: "Behind the green heights loom the blues; behind these the grays—all pinnacled against the skyglow thrusting up through gaps or behind promontories. Indescribably exquisite the foldings and hollowings of the emerald coast."

Approach any of the Antilles by sea today, and the same wind, the same colors and shapes greet you. The vision is all the more satisfying when you consider that some 16 generations of invaders, Europeans and Africans alike, have used these islands hard. For more than 300 years, the Spanish Main was a corridor and a staging area for the infestation of the New World by the Old. Gold-hungry conquistadors, rapacious buccaneers, planters, military men and adventurers came and went. The local Indians were systematically eliminated and replaced by thousands of shiploads of African slaves. The islands themselves were exploited, squabbled over, ravaged, mismanaged and populated in parts as densely as any lands on earth.

But the resilience of tropical environments is astonishing. Like robust courtesans blessed with good bone structure, the Antilles have never lost their power to enchant nor even, in certain lights, their virgin bloom. And—vastly more important to me—these islands contain an incredible number and variety of wild places.

Many of the islands, even those most densely populated, harbor pockets of wilderness too dry, too wet, too high or too remote to attract settlement. Recently I sought out these unspoiled islands within islands, traversing many a deserted shore. I probed rain forests on the high, wet flanks of mountainous Dominica; I swam through coral forests in the underwater landscapes off the shores of desert-dry Bonaire; I climbed through cloud banks on Hispaniola nearly two miles above sea level. To those whose image of the islands runs mainly to the quaint architecture, crumbling stone forts and sun-drenched beaches fringed with coconut palms, hibiscus and bougainvillaea (all, incidentally, plants brought here by Europeans) I can report that behind those façades there is still wilderness aplenty in the Antilles.

I had suspected as much since my first tantalizing glimpse of an unspoiled corner of the Caribbean in 1964. On a brilliant afternoon shortly after Christmas I sailed, all unprepared, into that luminous beauty and, like every pinched northern soul before me, I was transfixed. Actually, my family and I had flown from New York to Tortola (turtle) Island in the British Virgins, at the hinge of the Antilles where the island chain begins to bend southward. For the first part of the trip we were completely absorbed in changing planes and taking command of the 30-foot sloop and attendant dinghy that we had chartered for a fortnight. Not until we were several hours southward bound from Brandywine Bay did we relax enough to take a good look around. Ahead of us lay Deadman Bay on the north coast of little boomerang-shaped Peter Island, then virtually uninhabited—a vivid green mountaintop thrusting above the waves. Under us heaved the Caribbean, the same "flaming, dazzling lazulite" that Hearn had seen from the deck of his steam sailer in 1887.

Like Hearn, we were assaulted by color and light—and by another insistent force, a wind funneling at 20 knots down the Sir Francis Drake Channel, kicking up whitecaps and stuffing our sails.

It was the trade wind. To one who had shipped vicariously with Drake and Melville and had devoured Conrad, the words alone evoked the romance of the tropics. And so they should have. That soft, authoritative pressure on my cheek was the same wind that had blown hither the ships of Columbus and all who sailed in his wake. It is the wind that caresses these islands for most of the year, bringing day after day of mild bright weather with blue skies, fluffy cumulus clouds marching in endless parade, brief showers and then sunshine again.

As we approached Peter Island that Christmas season, the Antillean weather was at its finest. The wind held strong on our port quarter and it was easy sailing right up to the entrance of Deadman Bay. We decided to lower the sails and enter the unfamiliar anchorage under power, though in those crystal waters the passage through the reef was clearly visible. To eyes accustomed to the turbidity of Long Island Sound, the clarity of Caribbean water was incredible. When we dropped anchor I saw it sink through clouds of bubbles until it hit bottom three fathoms down. Then, as we drifted, the anchor line playing through my fingers, I watched the sparse turtle grass slip by under the hull. Here and there among the long, flat, dark-green fronds I spotted snails the size of baseballs and among them one bigger, horn-studded shell that I later learned was the abode of a queen conch.

This fascinating creature generally oozes along the sea floor at a snail's pace, peering around with golden-irised eyes set at the ends of long supple stalks; occasionally, by flexing its extended body, it makes abrupt underwater leaps and bounds. The islanders use its great conically twisted shell to make mellow, deep-toned horns and enthusiastically eat the meat inside. The queen conch, unhappily for its future in the Antilles, is among the world's largest and tastiest marine snails. Among Creole-speaking islanders it is called *lambi,* and if the name is not related in some distant way to the word lambaste, it should be, since before you can eat the animal you must pound the living hell out of the meat. In the hands of a skilled West Indian cook, it acquires the texture and taste of the finest veal.

A full-grown queen conch may inhabit a shell more than a foot long and weigh, shell and all, more than five pounds. But the heaviest shell does not necessarily shelter the largest animal. From time to time some irritating substance—a grain of sand, the larva of a marine worm or even a small shrimp—finds its way inside the shell. The conch responds by sheathing the intruder with secretions of mother-of-pearl, sometimes producing a pink pearl in the process, more often simply increasing the weight of the shell while decreasing the amount of room inside for the conch's organs and muscles. Eventually the overburdened conch, no longer able to drag itself around, expires—a victim, like some modern corporations and governments, of its own bulk.

Deadman Bay, our anchorage, is a shoaling cove whose sandy bottom, reflecting the sun, shows a pale and paler green graduating finally to the dazzling oyster white of the steep beach itself. The bay takes its name from an islet off the entrance called Deadman's Chest. There, Edward Teach, better known as Blackbeard the pirate, is said to have marooned 15 men with nothing more than a cutlass and a bottle of rum among them. To an avid childhood reader of Robert Louis Stevenson, "15 men on a dead man's chest" might have been reason enough to choose Deadman Bay for our first night's stay. But there was much more than that. Under the improbable, frazzled tops of arched coconut palms, some of whose rustling fronds reached lengths of 20 feet, a narrow strip of coral sand looped between two rocky points. And as far as we could see, there was not a footprint on it.

After anchoring, we plunged over the side and swam to shore. We walked the beach from end to end. There were, indeed, no footprints other than our own. But then we explored the fringing palm grove and found the canker in the rose. A complex of roads, invisible from the cove, had recently been bulldozed through the dense island growth, and as we followed one road for some distance uphill, it became apparent that this was the first step to an orderly grid development of Peter Island, and that someday soon the impossibly steep, green wall that backed our bay would be dotted with vacation homes.

Peter Island, we knew, had earlier been plowed for plantations, partially stripped of its trees and then gradually abandoned. The island had quickly reasserted itself, clothed once more in a dozen different shades of tropical green. The present mantle is shrubbier and less majestic, no doubt, than the island's virgin vestments—and one interwoven with trees and plants from Africa, Europe and the East Indies—but

Vivid flowers of the lobster claw heliconia plant thrust conspicuously from the greens of a watery glen on Dominica.

no less wild for all that. So when we found it, Peter Island was wilderness enough, and we soon discovered that the new roads made it easier for us to explore areas where otherwise we could not have penetrated 10 yards without swinging a machete. Our disappointment at having to share Peter Island with developers was forgotten when the sun set in an explosion of oranges, yellows and violets; and as if it were perched on the other end of a seesaw, the moon came up full.

After supper I rowed the dinghy ashore and walked alone the way we had gone that afternoon. It was a different world that I traveled through now. The rich primary colors of the afternoon had turned to shades of gray and the shadows on either side of the road were deep and forbidding. The rustle of palm fronds in the wind—the trade wind, still blowing a stiff 20 knots down the channel—sounded like falling rain. Overhead in silent zigzags flew bevies of bats feeding on gnats.

I came to the farthest point we had reached that afternoon, a hairpin turn halfway up the slope offering a clear view of Deadman Bay. In sunlight, the water's 20-foot depth had seemed no more than a thin watercolor wash of greens, blues and browns. Easily visible out by the reef, the long, flexible corals—aptly called gorgonians for their resemblance to the Gorgon's tresses—had swayed snakelike in the sea surge. Our toy sloop had appeared to be suspended in air, tethered by its sagging anchor line, the way a kite might look to a balloonist sailing by overhead. Now, though, with all lights turned out by those on board —in deference to the moon, no doubt—the sloop, dark against the silver sheen of Deadman Bay, seemed charged with pirate purpose.

Turning away, I climbed on toward the high, L-shaped ridge that formed the island's backbone. Half an hour later I stood near the ridge's highest point, 540 feet above the sea according to our nautical chart, and seemingly almost directly above it, so steeply did the land fall away. Actually, our bay was now hidden under a shoulder of the island. But here on the windswept ridge the thick vegetation that had hemmed me in on the road gave way to waist-high grasses, and I had a distant view in all directions. I found my gaze fixed to the northeast, smack into the wind that roared across my ears, and along a succession of featureless, monolithic shapes back-lighted by the moon.

Salt, Cooper, Ginger, Fallen Jerusalem, Virgin Gorda—those were the names man had given some of these islands. But where I looked, there were no lights or any other discernible works of man. I was inclined to accept the islands as they appeared in this primeval radiance, anonymous and unknown, much as they must have seemed to the first Europeans ever to penetrate this archipelago.

During the closing days of October 1492, with a brisk northeast wind at his back and with the Indian guides he had picked up in the Bahamas pointing the way, Christopher Columbus threaded the maze of low flat islands, cays and shallows now known as the Great Bahama Bank. Toward evening of the 27th, against darkening clouds on the horizon, he saw the hazy mass of Cuba. Eagerly, Columbus accepted the distant mountains and the ample estuary where he would drop anchor the next day as proof that by sailing west he had reached the eastern coast of Asia and the fabled Indies.

On later voyages Columbus would discover that Cuba was the largest and westernmost of a great chain of islands, but he never abandoned the conviction that the islands and the crystal sea they encompassed belonged, somehow, to the Indies. Later navigators proved otherwise, but Columbus' stubborn insistence had put the name Indies forever on the map. The region of this tropic sea, tucked between North and South America, became the West Indies. The islands are best known today as the Antilles, after the mythical island of Antilia, where legend says that Christians fleeing the Moorish invasion of the Iberian Peninsula in the Eighth Century took refuge. The sea itself was named Caribbean after the fiercest defenders of its islands, the Carib Indians.

The geologically oldest members of the Antillean family were formed about 150 million years ago. They are the four largest and are respectfully entitled the Greater Antilles. Just east of and second in size to Cuba is Hispaniola, physically divided by a lofty mountain range and divided politically into two countries, Haiti and the Dominican Republic. Flanking Hispaniola and roughly similar to each other in size and shape, are the two smallest of the big four, Jamaica on the west and Puerto Rico on the east.

At the eastern end of the Greater Antilles are the Virgin Islands, most of which are the protruding tops of mountains, part of a now-sunken land mass. Southeastward from the Virgins, the island chain becomes the Lesser Antilles—young islands, most of them, volcanic peaks that rose a mere 25 million years or so ago from a submerged plateau. This plateau, a sort of threshold between the Atlantic and the Caribbean, also supports an older, outer bastion of a few low, flat and dry limestone islands like Barbuda. The Lesser Antilles lie close together, the channels among them averaging no more than 25 miles in width, and most of them are oceanic, as opposed to continental, islands: some may, at times, have been connected with other islands, but none has ever been part of a continental land mass.

Columbus established the first European settlement in the New World on the north coast of Hispaniola in 1492, when the loss of his flagship, *Santa Maria,* forced him to leave 40 of his men behind. Indians soon killed all who had not already been murdered by their own messmates as a result of plots and quarrels. The setback was only temporary. The Spaniards returned in force. Within 50 years, nearly all the one million or more Arawak Indians on the Greater Antilles either had been massacred or had committed suicide to escape Spanish tyranny. Cattle, sheep and pigs, brought by the newcomers and allowed to run wild where there were no natural predators, proliferated prodigiously. Grazing, browsing, uprooting, trampling, they upset the natural balance over large portions of the islands. When the relatively small supply of gold in the Greater Antilles ran out and the early gold fever of the conquistadors abated somewhat, the true value of the islands became apparent. Fertile valley floors and coastal plains were cleared of vegetation and planted with vast fields of sugar cane and cotton.

The other half of the island chain, the Lesser Antilles—or the Caribbees, as they were also known—fared little better. When Columbus arrived in the West Indies he found the Carib Indians established as far north as the Virgin Islands and in the process of taking over the Antilles from the more civilized and placid Arawaks. The Caribs were the Huns of the West Indies. Stone-age barbarians, superb canoeists and swimmers, fighters who seemed to relish battle for its own sake, they had left the Orinoco Basin of South America to move north, island by island, killing and eating the Arawak males (the word Carib or Caribal is also the basis for the word cannibal) and enslaving the women to produce babies, which the Caribs also ate on occasion. These fearsome people soon acquired a taste for European flesh. An early historian even claimed that they made gourmet distinctions among nationalities, considering the French tastiest and the Spanish tough and indigestible. Despite their apparent advantage, the Spanish by and large ignored the Lesser Antilles for the simple reason that, whatever rewards the islands might offer, there was no gold there.

By the beginning of the 17th Century, however, other European powers had caught the colonial itch. The Lesser Antilles, gold barren but incredibly fertile and strategically valuable for controlling Caribbean trade routes, became hotly contested prizes. In the decade from 1666 to

1676, for example, the tiny island of St. Eustatius near the top of the Lesser Antilles changed hands five times among the Dutch, the English and the French, and supported a population of 20,000.

The Caribs remained a threat to life and limb (literally, since they customarily smoked the arms and legs of their victims to preserve the meat for later consumption) until well into the 19th Century, by which time they had been pushed off all the islands but St. Vincent and Dominica. A 7,300-acre Carib reserve still exists on Dominica, but the Carib blood of its 500 inhabitants has been much diluted by European and African infusions, and the Carib language is largely forgotten.

Not all the islands, even after being cleared of Indians, became so thickly settled as St. Eustatius, but almost every island considered even remotely fit for development was exploited down to the last profitable square foot. The process extended to islands like Saba, a steep-sided volcanic cone near St. Eustatius with hardly a level acre and no port or beach, and even to tiny dots like Peter Island, where I now stood.

The wilderness has recaptured thousands of plantations, even whole islands, as we learned during the next two weeks. We saw many lovely and deserted beaches and swam with snorkels and masks over reefs where the fish showed little fear. And in later years we sailed to other unspoiled islands in this sea. But for me the promise of that night on Peter Island, the vision of being at the heart of an untainted tropical paradise, was not fulfilled until I set out upon my most recent quest.

Some of the many Antillean wildernesses I visited proved to be wildly and wonderfully at variance with my preconceptions of paradise, but each had its peculiar enchantment. Take, for example, Barbuda. I went there because I had heard it was the most remote and least-visited island of appreciable size in the Antilles, because it was a prime example of a low, dry Antillean island, because of its unique and fascinating history and because it was the site of the only remaining frigate-bird rookery in the eastern Caribbean (pages 36-49).

I flew to Antigua, then changed to a twin-engined, 10-passenger plane for the 20-minute flight to Barbuda, where, in good time, I found myself spending a night on the island's deserted eastern shore. I had never slept out of doors in the tropics before, except on the decks of sailboats, and then always off a lee shore or in some sheltered cove like Deadman Bay. So I was quite unprepared for the cold—doubly uncomfortable here where the stiff northeast trade wind that blew through the night could gnaw at me from both flanks and from the top and bot-

Seen across the calm and narrow inlet to English Harbor on Antigua in the Leeward Islands, a sinking sun tints clouds, sea and sky.

tom too. My total exposure was due to being bedded down—or up—in a hammock slung from the ceiling of a shallow cave partway up the face of a limestone cliff and opening into the teeth of the wind. The cotton mesh hammock was a direct descendant of the ones Columbus had discovered the island Indians using. My decision to carry it in place of a sleeping bag had been fortified by the glowing report of a 16th Century Spanish Dominican missionary, Bartolomé de las Casas.

"Hammocks," which Las Casas explained came from the Indian word *hamaca,* are "attached to the posts of the houses, and thus are off the ground and swing in the air; and as the good ones are three and four *varas* (8 to 11 feet) and more in width, one opens them when they swing as we should open a very big sling, putting oneself in diagonally as in an angle; and thus there is the rest of the hammock with which to cover oneself, and that is sufficient because it is never cold. It is very restful to sleep in."

The good father was right on the last point. My hammock was comfortable enough. But cover myself with it I could not, being a bit short on *varas,* I guess, and it *was* cold. With only a tissue-thin nylon poncho to wrap up in and no more clothes than the shirt and shorts I had set out in that morning from Codrington, Barbuda's only town, I was forced to clamber out of the big sling every couple of hours to stoke my driftwood fire and drive the chill out of my bones.

The wind that was chilling me now was, I reflected wryly, a child of the sun, in a relationship suspected as early as 1700 by another Dominican missionary, Père Jean-Baptiste Labat, who spent 12 years in the French West Indies and commented exhaustively on the natural history of the region. "It is by no means by chance," he wrote in his monumental journal *Nouveau Voyage aux Iles de l'Amérique,* "that the trade winds exist in the Torrid Zone, since their cause is an inevitable, infallible and unceasing one, arising as it does either from the movement of the earth around the Sun, or from the movement of the Sun around the earth." Though shaky on astronomy, Labat knew his physics. The sun heats the earth most where its rays fall most directly—at the equator. The tropical sea of air, growing hottest around the equator, expands and rises. Cooler air from the poles flows in under it. As these winds approach the equatorial regions, the rotation of the earth bends them westward, producing the northeast and southeast trades—the steadiest, most persistent winds on earth.

Through most of the year the cool, dry northeast trade wind lavishes upon the Antilles the near-perfect weather for which the Caribbean is famous. Temperatures seldom vary more than a few degrees from the annual average of about 80° F. Occasionally a northerly, a winter wind escaped from the Temperate Zone, sweeps down with high seas and low temperatures, but by and large Caribbean weather shuns extremes and changes its moods gradually and predictably. Even its most violent aberrations, hurricanes, are looked for only in certain months. A seamen's mnemonic proverb makes the point: June, too soon/July, stand by/August, you must/September, remember/October, all over.

The trade wind dies in the Antilles only in midsummer, the days of the doldrums. Then, the northeast and southeast trades meet near the equator and create a region of squalls, calms and variable airs difficult to sail through and a nursery for thunderstorms and hurricanes. Temperatures in the Antilles rise, though the moderating effect of the sea keeps them from soaring. Thunderstorms become more frequent and Antilleans begin to watch their barometers for signs of hurricanes.

But now it was the Ides of March. The doldrums were still 1,000 miles south of Barbuda. On the morning that I set out from Codrington, the trade wind kept me cool and dry as I trudged along under a 50-pound pack, although the temperature was in the 80s. A comparable effort on an 80° F. day in Maine would have left me dripping.

A quarter of the weight of that pack represented drinking water, for there was none that I knew of on my side of the island, and at this time of year Barbuda could count on no rain except for an occasional brief shower trailed by an errant squall. High volcanic peaks on islands like Dominica, Guadeloupe and Grenada force incoming clouds to rise into cooler air and shed their moisture in drenching daily downpours, but here, for months to come, all plant and animal life would have to hoard every drop of water. Already the frangipani trees had dropped most of their leaves; among the surrounding evergreens they looked half dead.

It appeared that today I would have the windward coast entirely to myself. Divers from Codrington do come here to spearfish and to hunt lobsters, but usually they walk along the same six-mile road that I was taking, and the only footprints I saw in the powdery dust, untouched by rain for days, were those of ground doves, donkeys and lizards.

One could assume such isolation on Barbuda because of the island's unusual history. Unlike most of the other sizable Antilles, Barbuda, nearly six times as large as St. Eustatius, had never been subdivided. Throughout the colonial period it had remained the personal domain of a single family. In 1685, Charles II of England approved letters patent

Spanish explorers and native islanders flee the fury of a Caribbean hurricane in this late 16th Century engraving. The awful havoc wrought by the storm, according to an accompanying Latin caption, included trees "ripped up by the roots" and the devastating loss of three ships that "went down to the bottom together with all hands."

granting Barbuda to Christopher and John Codrington, wealthy planters who also owned estates on Barbados and Antigua. When Queen Anne renewed the Crown's grant 20 years later, the terms provided that the Codringtons were to pay "unto Her Majesty yearly and every year one Fat Sheep if demanded." Though no record exists that a sheep ever actually changed hands, the Codrington family ruled Barbuda well into the second half of the 19th Century.

By then its pattern of settlement had been well established. The entire population of several hundred blacks and a few white overseers lived in a town named, predictably, Codrington. The town lay close to Barbuda's only harbor—wide, shallow Codrington Lagoon on the protected Caribbean side of the island. Barbuda's soil was too thin and its climate too dry for the cultivation of cash crops, so the Codringtons used the island primarily for raising cattle, horses, donkeys and slaves. Later on, they added fallow deer, goats, wild boar, grouse and other imported game, making the island also a private hunting preserve for the family and their friends. Some game still warily roams the flat scrublands today, but unless one visits the frigate-bird rookery in the mangrove swamps of Codrington Lagoon, the animals one is most likely to see are feral horses, donkeys and cattle.

The Codringtons profitably exported Barbudan hides, tallow, smoked beef and sea salt to the other islands and strong young field hands to the family sugar-cane plantations in Antigua. When slavery was abolished throughout the British Empire in 1834, the Codrington heirs met their reversal of fortune manfully. They permitted the island's blacks to remain in their wattle-and-daub huts, which clustered around the port. But they made it quite clear that without the permission of the estate manager nobody could graze goats, plant taro roots or yams, hunt or build a hut beyond the boundaries of the little settlement. They even restricted fishing and the taking of crab or lobster in Barbudan waters. Thus for a time the Codringtons were assured that the blacks remaining on the island—and there was no way to leave save on Codrington boats—must continue to work for their former owners if they wanted to eat. When even this system failed to yield enough profit to run the island, the Codringtons surrendered their lease to the British Crown.

The 1,145 islanders are now permitted to plant crops, though there is precious little soil fit for that, and to graze their goats on Crown lands —but not to own or build on any land outside the town limits. There is only one hotel, perched on the island's far southern tip. Beyond Codrington, one can roam for days on end without coming upon another person or a habitation.

So when I reached the windward shore of Barbuda, with the coastline stretching away north and south of me until it faded from sight in a surf-spawned haze, I had no reason to suppose that along its entire length there stood another soul but me. Before me lay a choppy lagoon, 10 to 15 feet deep and from a few hundred yards to half a mile wide. Beyond the lagoon, the wind-driven waves of the Atlantic Ocean crashed in white plumes on a barely submerged coral reef. Reefs are a trademark of windward coasts, where coral, which depends on the movement of the sea to bring it food, grows more vigorously than on calm leeward shores. Easing my pack onto the sand, I dug out flippers, snorkel and a hand spear and set out to reconnoiter the seaward half of my domain. Swimming through the lagoon was easy except when I had to battle a strong lateral current running toward a break in the reef, where the water that had piled over the coral wall found its exit. The inner side of the reef, I discovered, was split and divided into a maze of underwater canyons, corridors and caves, over the tops of which the breaking surf rolled in effervescent clouds. In this nourishing, turbulent pasture, a myriad of fishes fed on plankton, on coral polyps—and on one another. Feeling very much an intruder, I nevertheless foraged there too, impaling a silver chub that I later ate for supper.

I swam back through the calmer waters of the lagoon to the shore, which alternated between beaches of fine, white coral sand and an abrupt, dark gray coral shelf. This crenelated mass evidently was a dead, dry replica of the outer reef, the result of a 10-foot drop in sea level—or an equivalent elevation of the land—thousands of years ago. The beach led up to a narrow, pitted limestone terrace, supporting in its cracks and potholes a prickly assemblage of cacti, agaves (sisal), leathery-leafed evergreen shrubs and other salt-tolerant and drought-resistant plants. Then came a tumble of giant, razor-sharp slabs and blocks of ancient coral that had broken loose from, and fallen to, the base of a 100-foot cliff. A quarter of a million years ago waves like those now smashing against the outer reef had left the cliff face pocked with hundreds of niches, holes and even respectably sized caves.

From among a number of promising-looking apertures I finally chose one of the larger ones about a quarter of the way up the cliff. Climbing up the jagged coral, even with my pack, was as easy as scaling the ladder to a loft. In fact, although the cave was 80 feet wide and 20 feet high at the opening, its ceiling sloping back to meet the gradually rising floor, in that giant landscape it gave the same cosy feeling as the loft of a barn. From it I had a view over the beach, the lagoon, the reef and the Atlantic to the wall of cumulus clouds on the horizon.

During the afternoon I made several trips to the beach to gather fuel for the fire that I expected to use chiefly for cooking. Driftwood was plentiful and I lugged back up to my cave quite a pile of it—more, I decided, than I would ever be able to use. Between trips I enjoyed the company of a persistent visitor—a hummingbird. I do not believe the tiny creature lived in my cave, but the cavern was certainly part of its regular beat. Throughout the afternoon the bird showed up at intervals of about 20 minutes. I always saw it silhouetted against a bright sky or in the dim light of the cave, so I could not be certain of its species or its colors, except that they were dark. I invariably heard it before I saw it; there were three sharp metallic notes, like the sound of steel balls striking together. The coral strand provided no flowers or nectar for this fellow. It appeared to feed on insects picked off the walls of the cave. On first arriving, it would sit on a frangipani branch outside, peering intently up toward the cave ceiling. Then in a flash it would be inside, hovering just inches away from the roof, darting, hovering, darting again. I never could identify exactly what it feasted on.

At the end of the day the clouds on the horizon turned rose pink, while unseen behind me, on the other side of the island, the sun was setting. Then the color drained away, leaving the clouds a smoky blue, and at that moment two small hawks appeared, first one and then its mate. Evidently I had usurped their home. They perched on the top of a huge chunk of fallen coral almost level with the lip of the cave. Each made a pass inside, landing for an instant in a crevice in the ceiling. Then each swooped out again. Clearly, they did not care to share their cave. For nearly half an hour, as the light faded, they continued to consider the matter, occasionally screeching their frustration at me. Then they flew off—perhaps to some other cave or wave-hollowed niche.

By the time the stars appeared in the darkening sky, I was already feeling thankful that I had carried so much driftwood up from the beach. I shivered and huddled in my hammock next to the fire through the night. When first light finally came at about 5:30, I was wide awake. At 6 a.m. I rolled out of my hammock for the fourth time and put the last wood on the fire. By 6:15 the sun still had not appeared, but my hummingbird was up and working, searching the cave walls and ceiling for breakfast. Then the hawks reappeared and perched on the same boulder from which they had scolded me the night before. They were still preening, ridding themselves perhaps of the dust of some unfamiliar refuge, when the sun finally flashed vertical shafts from behind the tops of the clouds massed on the horizon. And then came the first wedge of orange fire; my cave took on a rosy hue. I could feel the warmth right away. The earth was still turning around the sun—or the sun around the earth, I cared not which. The trade wind blew as steadily as ever. It was the beginning of another Caribbean day, marvelously like the last.

Barbuda's Amorous Pirates

PHOTOGRAPHS BY JOHN DOMINIS

In a salty lagoon on the northwest corner of the island of Barbuda lies an enormous rookery inhabited by one of the most fascinating bird species anywhere. This is home for the frigate bird—*Fregata magnificens*, alias man-o'-war bird—an aerial pirate of supreme daring, a flyer of consummate skill and a lover whose feathery flirtations rival Casanova's.

Barbuda's colony numbers some 5,000 adult birds, a thriving population supported in large part by the rich supply of fish on the Barbuda Bank, a reef lying only eight miles west of the frigate's rookery. Eight miles is hardly more than a wing's flap or two for a bird of the frigate's awesome skill and physical structure. With an eight-foot wingspread and only a three-pound body weight, the frigate has a wingspan-to-weight ratio greater than any other flying creature except for some hummingbirds. Unlike those frenzied flappers, however, the frigate lazily soars on air currents that may take it as high as 2,000 feet, where the bird glides for hours searching for food.

When the frigate spots a potential meal near the surface, it plummets, grabs the fish or squid and soars again, having barely touched the water. Because its feathers do not bear the protective oily impregnation common to those of most other sea birds, the frigate bird must be adept at feeding on the wing. When mischance does put the frigate in the sea, it must take off quickly or become waterlogged.

When food hunting, the piratical frigate prefers to scout the beaches. Midair hijacking provides it with another source of nourishment. On such missions two or more frigates will gang up and cruise till they find a slower-flying bird that has just caught a fish. Then one frigate peels off to chase the quarry, matching maneuvers zig for zag and sometimes capsizing the victim in flight. When the terrorized bird drops its prize —or disgorges the partly digested morsel from its gullet—one of the other frigates snares the secondhand tidbit before it hits the water.

Second only to a frigate bird's concern for food is its interest in the opposite sex. The mating season begins near the end of summer when the males make it their business to find new mates and set up housekeeping. As the photographs on the following pages reveal, the courtship and domestic rituals of frigate birds are every bit as elaborate as those of that other pirate species: man.

A posturing male frigate pumps up his fetching scarlet neck pouch with air and waits for an unattached hen to pass by. A badge of bachelorhood, the pouch gets its color from pigment and a dense network of capillaries that becomes engorged with blood as the bird's ardor begins to rise.

A Success with a Passing Lady

Courtship among Barbuda's frigates reaches a peak about the beginning of November. During the pre-mating ritual, each sex carries out a strictly patterned role. Among frigate birds, it is the females who do the conspicuous searching out and selecting of mates. The hens take to the air above the rookery to look over the males, who cluster in groups ranging from four to about 20 atop the lagoon's scrubby mangrove bushes.

Whenever a female shows some interest in a group of males—indicated by hesitating in flight or circling over their mangrove bush—the males react with a colorful and blatant display of wooing. They tilt their heads far back to show off their fully inflated scarlet pouches. They vibrate their wings rapidly back and forth. And to further entice the females, they emit various clicking and drumming sounds.

Alas, such ardor is no guarantee of quick success. Hens may serenely overfly group after group of amorous males before settling on mates. Ignored on their original perches, the ever-hopeful male suitors will often flap from one mangrove bush to another, their still-inflated pouches wobbling awkwardly. Eventually, however, most of the male birds do manage to attract a female's attention and get themselves selected. And after other rituals to confirm the bond, some of which involve mutual touching, the pair is ready to settle down to start a family.

A male, pouch fully blown, flaps mightily to attract passing hens.

An interested hen swoops by for a quick inspection of the courtier.

The hen lands and takes a long, close look at the displaying male.

Almost committed to her selected male, the hen settles inside his embracing wing as the satisfied suitor begins to emit purring sounds.

In the final stages of courtship, two frigate birds rub their necks together and periodically interlock their rapidly opening and closing bills. Such intimacies help the birds to recognize each other in the rookery's bustle.

Newly mated birds also rub against each other in a kind of mutual shimmy. Although the male's pouch is now partly deflated, it will puff up again during the next few weeks. After egg laying it will deflate altogether.

A mother frigate flies off her recently laid egg for an extended feeding foray.

The male arrives to brood the egg, pouch now deflated.

On the nest, the male rolls the egg over to ensure that it is evenly warmed.

After several days, the mother returns to relieve the male.

Well-tended Home for a Chick

In the structured world of the frigate bird, it is the male's job to find twigs for the nest. This is not easy, for mangrove branches are hard to break and loose twigs are widely sought. The piratical frigates do not hesitate to rob neighboring nests for materials, so the females stay home to guard the nest.

Both mother and father take long turns brooding the egg, never leaving it unattended. Yet as much as 65 per cent of the eggs never hatch: other frigates may crack them while trying to rob the nest of twigs, the parents accidentally knock some to the ground during brooding chores and some eggs fall through the shakily constructed nests.

If the egg survives, after about 50 days' incubation the chick hatches, naked and defenseless. Both parents continue to tend it for five or six weeks not only to feed it but also to protect it from attacks by other frigates and to shield it from the sun until it has grown a coat of fine down. Thereafter, the parents visit the baby bird only at feeding time.

Almost four more months pass before the chick is ready to fly. Long before this, however, the father has departed, leaving his mate to feed the chick while it is experimenting with flight. During this period the chick also learns to fish. But because the frigate's fishing technique is difficult, young birds lose weight during their apprenticeship and would starve without the mother's help.

This chick would die of exposure or be hurt by marauders without parental protection.

A formation of soaring frigates—including a white-headed adolescent flying at the lower right—skims over a crowded mangrove clump.

An Island's Watery Aerodrome

The swampy area that Barbuda's frigates inhabit is ideally placed and equipped to act as an aerodrome for the birds. The mangrove bushes in which the birds build their nests rise some six to eight feet above the mud-flats—just right to serve as launching pads. Furthermore, the mangroves' springy branches provide a boost for takeoff. This is essential, since over the course of evolution, the legs of these aerial masters have degenerated to the point where they are almost useless in assisting any attempted takeoff from level ground.

Another aerodynamic plus for the mangrove swamp is the fact that it is situated on the side of the lagoon that is exposed to the trade winds. The fresh breeze not only helps the frigates to take off easily—upwind, of course—but also to land at slow speeds and with pinpoint accuracy. Landing precision is a necessary skill, for a frigate's runway is often merely a thin branch encumbered by a madly begging chick, and swaying in a 15-knot wind. Adding to these difficulties is the fact that the crowded rookery contains an average of three nests in every 9-by-12-foot section—tight quarters for a bird with an eight-foot wingspread.

Given this lack of wing room, it is not surprising that frigate rookeries are noisy, contentious places where the birds are constantly arguing about something: landing rights, perch ownership, nesting sites and who owns which twig.

Angrily clacking, two neighboring frigates drive a marauder away from their curious chicks. Chicks quickly adopt the adults' disputatious

A partly feathered chick, backed by its father, helps rebuff an unwelcome visitor.

behavior and before long are noisily holding their own.

A swooping young frigate tries vainly to steal a twig from the nest of an older bird.

Sunset tints the Caribbean sky over Barbuda as hordes of frigates swarm down on their rookery to spend the night. After a final flurry of

noisy dispute, the birds will settle down quietly; only the plaintive call of the young nestlings begging for food will disrupt the silence.

2/ The Inner World of Dominica

*The denseness of the forest opened
into a loosely connected system of dells and great clumps
of creeper-hung trees, a vague, steaming
and antediluvian world.* PATRICK LEIGH FERMOR/ THE TRAVELLER'S TREE

West Indians say there is only one island in the Antilles that Columbus would still recognize: Dominica, member of the British Commonwealth and third largest of the Lesser Antilles. On the night of Saturday, November 2, 1493, the Admiral of the Ocean Sea, on his second voyage to the New World, felt strongly that he was nearing land. He ordered his armada of 17 ships to heave to until morning. Sunday's daylight revealed a heavily forested island rising abruptly from the sea, its lofty interior a jumble of crinkled valleys and ridges.

Columbus noted the lack of suitable anchorage, named the island Dominica (Spanish for Sabbath) and sailed past it north toward blue shapes that beckoned on the horizon. Later, legend says, when the King and Queen of Spain asked their admiral to describe his discovery, he crumpled a piece of parchment in his two hands and held it out to them. That, he said, is how the land lies. The land still lies much as it did then: mountainous, forested, with no barrier reefs, no lagoon to shelter ships and no tourist-tempting miles of broad white beaches. It is so isolated from the mainstream of Antillean development that its inhabitants call themselves "the people who live behind God's back."

To 17th Century colonizers, however, Dominica held promise. Strategically located between the French islands of Guadeloupe to the north and Martinique to the south, it was fertile and almost excessively well watered. Incessant rains soaked the slopes of the volcanic chain that forms the island's spine. A network of rivers cut the island into lush valleys and offered an abundance of foot-long crayfish and crabs. There were birds and small game aplenty in the forests, and even a large and deliciously edible frog unique to the island.

Unfortunately for the European settlers, the island also harbored tough Caribs who called the place Waitubukuli, meaning Scene of Big Battles, presumably in memory of their massacres of the previous tenants, the Arawaks. The Caribs attacked Europeans with equal ferocity, impartially slaughtering the British and the French, who alternately fought each other and the Caribs for possession of this vital link in the French island chain. For more than a century, Frenchmen and Britons continued their squabbling, raiding back and forth against settlements and fortifications. Only through the Treaty of Versailles of 1783 did Britain gain definitive possession of Dominica—though French place names like Grande Soufrière, Anse Bateaux and Perdu Temps still outnumber English ones. The Caribs, for their part, fought on, but with diminishing effect. Their lands preempted by plantation owners, their blood increasingly mixed through intermarriage with imported black slaves, they gradually declined in numbers. In 1903 their British overlords settled them on a 7,300-acre reservation where they could carry on a semblance of their old tribal ways. About 500 Caribs live there today, though only a few are of pure descent.

Dominica's rugged resistance to domestication—sensed by Columbus and experienced by generations of French and British planters—is what attracted me to the island. I flew there from Barbuda, and the contrast with that flat, dry island was overwhelming. I understood at once what Alec Waugh meant when he wrote of Dominica: "I had not believed that anything could be so green."

For several weeks I immersed myself in the island's green immensity, staying first in a fishing village on the rock-bound northeast coast, probably within sight of the spot where Columbus had lain-to for the night. Later I moved to the lush hills above the capital of Roseau, settling in Island House, a comfortable hostelry run by an American couple, Peter and Margery Brand. From this base I explored the inner recesses of Dominica, guided by the experiences of the Brands (who had come to the island in 1961), by forest rangers and by a silent but highly informative companion that I bought in Roseau.

The latter was a copy of the British topographical DOS (Directorate of Overseas Surveys) map of Dominica, scale 1 to 50,000. This map shows an irregular oval like the silhouette of a knobby Idaho potato, 29 miles from north to south and 16 miles from east to west. Solid red lines trace the course of "main roads." On Dominica, "main" means little more than that two ordinary vehicles can pass each other. There are not many such roads. Two of them intersect in a forest clearing near the center of the island; the others hug the coast. The rest of the island is accessible by tracks or footpaths, represented on the map by thin, dotted black lines. Many more tracks and footpaths are not shown at all. I know because I tramped them.

One such path leads to the forbiddingly named Valley of Desolation southeast of 4,400-foot Morne Trois Pitons, the more southerly of Dominica's two tallest mountains. Trois Pitons and 4,747-foot Morne Diablotin, rising from either end of a high central plateau, are extinct volcanoes, but the region of the Valley of Desolation is still simmering and as recently as 1880 was shaken by a tremendous blast of steam. The valley is one of the island's scenic wonders; but very few of the Dominicans I talked to had seen it, perhaps because its volcanic vapors are alleged to have killed at least one visitor.

Three other Island House guests and I set out for the valley one morning before dawn. Dennis McCloire, hunter and guide, led the way up through a region botanists call elfin woodland, a low canopy of stunted, moss-draped trees, twisted and dwarfed by wind and the cooler temperatures of high altitude. The growth was so dense that Dennis had to hack a trail through it with his machete. (Dominicans call this handy tool a cutlass, perhaps a holdover from pirate days, and never go into the forest without one.)

We burst from this prison of roots and limbs to stare several hundred feet down a crumbling concave precipice. Dennis, first to the edge, lost his hat to a sudden, errant blast from the trade wind that had swooped up and out of the giant depression below us, carrying the stench of sulfur. As the rest of us peered over the edge we saw a sight strange on Dominica: a great expanse of bare earth, like an enormous gravel pit. With each blast of wind came the high-pitched roar of escaping steam. Jets of vapor rose here and there on the valley floor.

We picked our way carefully down a steep, raw slope. Water oozed out of the mountainside. For part of the way, we navigated a steep water-cut gutter, bracing ourselves against the two sides. At the bottom we found ourselves at the head of the valley. Steam and hot water billowed and bubbled out of the ground around us. I soon got used to the stench, but not to the unique feeling of openness, so different from all other sensations on this densely vegetated island. The sulfurous fumes, swept up the face of the basin by the trade wind, prevent the growth of all but a few tough grasses, lichens and creamy-flowered terrestrial bromeliads. Here it was possible to see, better than anywhere else on the island, just how a typical Dominican river begins. Out of the raw, rain-sodden soil percolated little rivulets of water, collecting and swelling and running together and finally, all in one stream, cutting their way out of the natural basin to tumble over rocks and boulders as a full-fledged brook named the Coldwater. Though fed by thermal springs, the Coldwater was indeed cold compared to a stream it meets a mile from its source. This second stream comes from a thermal cul-de-sac of its own, this one as hot as the hottest bearable bath; before we left that day I soaked in it under the sun, sweating happily.

A few days later I made an equally wet but chillier trip with a forest ranger named Bernard Jean-Baptiste. J-B, as everyone called him, led me to the larger of the island's two real lakes, Boeri, in the mountains behind Laudat, his natal village. The climb up to the old volcanic crater in which Lake Boeri lies was through a dank tangle of moss-covered trees—many, like the *mangle blanc,* a kind of inland mangrove, perched on spidery aerial roots that help support them in the mucky soil.

The tree trunks were festooned with climbing vines and scrambler lianas called *zelle-mouches* in Creole because their long, narrow, corrugated leaves literally look like flies' wings. The local hunters, who still prowl Dominica's forested slopes, use them to thatch temporary lean-tos. Beneath the trees grew ordinary ferns taller than my head, tree ferns 30 feet high and wild ginger, whose fragrant white flower was one of the few visible in the forest at this season. Another was a bright red lobster claw heliconia, or *balisier;* its broad leaves, about five feet long, make good umbrellas. According to Père Labat, a Carib warrior intent on ambushing an enemy would cover himself with vegetation and top off his camouflage with a *balisier* leaf through which he punched two eyeholes.

J-B and I crossed a dozen little streams. Toward the end of our march the trail itself became a watercourse. When we reached the lake, I peered through the tangled undergrowth at a body of water about half a mile across and entirely surrounded by forest. There was no indication of any shore. J-B said he had never seen the lake so full at this time of year. Now, in the dry season, the level ought to have been 100 feet lower, exposing a border of mud flats through which one could walk around the lake. Instead we had to inch our way through a dense thicket of shrubs and roots that sprouted between slippery boulders.

The only way I could get a proper look at the lake was to swim. Fifty yards out in the cold gray-green water I lost sight of J-B. Beneath me were eerie, wavering shapes that I guessed to be boulders and submerged shrubs. The heavy green walls of the old crater pressed in on the lake on all sides. I swam back to land with quick strokes.

The next morning J-B and I set out on a different sort of expedition, heading for Gros Bois, a forest in the Clyde Valley above the airport on the windward coast. J-B hoped that there we might catch a glimpse of a *sisserou* or a *jacquot,* the island's two indigenous parrots, which have been hunted almost to the point of extinction. The *sisserou,* or imperial parrot, is the largest of the parrot genus *Amazona.* It is a magnificent bird, nearly two feet high with a royal-purple front, greenish-blue wings and a dark violet band running across the back of its neck.

We never actually reached the area marked Gros Bois on the map, but after leaving our car in a coconut grove we climbed to within a few miles of it through a government-protected forest reserve above the Fire Flint Ravine. This was primary rain forest, the "optimal formation," according to the American botanist W. H. Hodge, who claims that "nowhere in the American tropics can a better display of it be seen than in the interior of Dominica."

We walked at a museum pace along a hunters' trail that meandered among giant trees. A hundred feet above our heads a seamless green canopy seemed to rest on massive pillars—the smooth columns of *gommiers* (gum trees) and the reddish, rough-barked trunks of *châtaigniers* (chestnut trees). A *châtaignier* is unmistakable, spreading at its base into buttresses that extend from the tree's axis and curve like drapery on an enormous statue. The *gommier* is plainer, more severe. Rapped with the knuckles, it gives the feel of solid rock. Hacked with a machete, it oozes the resinous, highly flammable gum that gives the tree its name and is most useful in kindling fires in the forest.

Besides those two dominants, J-B pointed out a host of other large trees. In one typical 10-acre patch of primary rain forest on Dominica, Hodge counted 60 species of trees. An equal-sized tract of Temperate Zone forest might have no more than a dozen. The tropics, whether in the rain forest or on a coral reef, tend to support many different species in moderate numbers. The Temperate Zone gives rise to relatively few species, though often in vast numbers. It is easier, evidently, for the oddball to survive in the more congenial climate of the tropics.

Sulfurous fumes surging up through crevices in crumbling volcanic rock lend the look of an inferno to Dominica's Valley of Desolation.

Bois cote, mahot cochon, zyeux crabbe, laurier blanc: I savored their euphonious Creole names but could no more keep them straight than if J-B had been introducing me to a roomful of strangers. One of them, however, its bark speckled with whitish warts, was easier to remember than the rest—*bois diable,* "wood of the devil." The tree may have been named for its warts or for the hardness of its wood, excellent for making charcoal, but a devil of a job to cut.

The bewildering variety of trees J-B was naming supported in their crowns a whole kingdom of air and parasitic plants, as well as birds, bats, toads, snakes, lizards and insects that live almost entirely out of touch with the ground. Even the tree frogs, requiring water to complete their life cycle as amphibians, find miniature pools in the cabbage-like leaves of various bromeliads. Up there, 100 feet above our heads, in bright sunshine or in heavy rain, was a rich, teeming biological zone. To that height vines and scrambling plants aspire, and from it the extraordinary plant called the clusia, or *kaklin,* sends down its hawser-like roots. These vegetable probes seem particularly strange to one used to plants whose parts grow smaller as they grow longer. Hanging straight down 75 feet and more from the branches of the forest trees, the *kaklin* roots maintain virtually the same width at the top as at the bottom, anywhere from macaroni-sized to as big around as a man's forearm. When they reach the ground they take root and begin to grow in girth. Those an inch or so in diameter, when not yet rooted or when sliced through, make perfect ropes for swinging Tarzan-style.

Parrots and other birds that feed on the figlike fruit of the *kaklin* drop the seeds high in the crowns of trees. There they germinate, subsisting at first on whatever vegetative litter—dead leaves and the like —lies around them. When this food supply runs out the *kaklin* begins lowering its life lines. After the first root has reached the ground the plant begins to grow more vigorously, sending down more and more tentacles as long as the host tree remains standing. Often the *kaklin* causes its own downfall by getting so heavy that it brings the tree's crown crashing to the earth, *kaklin* and all.

Still hoping to spot a *sisserou,* J-B and I sat quietly for a time on some protruding roots of a *châtaignier,* listening. As usual, there came the flutelike song of the shy mountain whistler and the sharp metallic voices of unseen hummingbirds. Below, in the valley, we could hear undertones of the Fire Flint River on its way to join the Clyde and the Atlantic. Now and again all sound was overwhelmed when a gust of wind swept through the treetops far overhead. A large hawk—J-B called it a chicken hawk—sailed through the high branches in an exhibition of stunt flying that, for so large a bird, hardly seemed possible. We were about to move on when we heard at last the trilling squawk of a parrot —a *jacquot*, J-B thought. Our hopes rose, but although we heard parrots call several more times that day, we never spotted a live one. The green plumage touched with shades of orange and brilliant blue, which makes parrots such ornamental pets, renders them nearly invisible in the forest canopy. On our way out, however, we came upon a melancholy scattering of orange, green, blue and brown feathers around the remains of a campfire—two *jacquots* and a *sisserou*, J-B reckoned. Since 1914 the parrots have been protected by law. So when hunters shoot them now, they eat them in the forest.

Back in my room at Island House that night I reached a decision about a matter that had been looming steadily larger on my personal horizon, like clouds piling up around the head of massive Morne Diablotin. Indeed, much of my thinking had to do with those very clouds.

No one had ever taken the pains to measure accurately the total annual rainfall on the upper slopes of Diablotin, but reliable estimates have put it at around 400 inches a year. That mountaintop must be the wettest spot in the Caribbean and among the wettest on earth. It is hard to say exactly how many rivers begin on Diablotin's slopes, but they must number close to a dozen, depending on one's definition of a river, all running off in different directions to the sea. The largest is the Layou, which gathers its waters from the southeastern flank of the Diablotin. Flowing past an upland village called Bells, the river turns west into uninhabited country and, as if in a hurry to reach the sea, slices down through the volcanic rock ribs of the island, dropping 700 feet in four miles. Toward the latter half of this chute, the river's banks become vertical cliffs rising from boulder-strewn cascades and deep, slow-moving pools. In places the cliffs reach heights of 500 feet and more and are topped by virgin rain forest rising another 100 feet. This is the Layou River gorge. Because there are no major waterfalls, it is possible to descend the gorge in a day, half swimming and half clambering over rocks. Local fishermen know ways up and down the steep walls. For the uninitiate who enters the gorge at Bells, however, there is no safe exit until he reaches a suspension footbridge five miles downstream, just above the point where the river spills out onto the narrow coastal plain. From the footbridge a short path leads to a main road.

Peter and Margery Brand and three friends had made the trip through the gorge during the dry season five years before. Others must have preceded them in the course of Dominican history, but there is no record of the fact, so the Brands consider themselves pioneers. They spoke with wonder of the narrow river pools cupped between fern-draped walls, so deep and still that it seemed impossible the pools were part of any river. If you want to plumb the island primeval, they said, go there.

The Brands had urged me not to make the trip alone and I had tried (halfheartedly, I now concede) to find someone to go with me. I had even put off the trip twice because people who said they wanted to go were unable at the last minute to make it. Tomorrow was my last day on Dominica, my last chance to descend the Layou. I would have to do it alone or not at all. With a growing lightness of heart, I finally admitted to myself that I really longed to be off on my own at last, to reach the heart of this wild island and to be the only one there.

There were dangers. But it hardly seemed that they would be much diminished by my having company. The worst that could happen, the Brands explained, was to be caught in the gorge when the river flooded. I already knew by heart an ominous passage in W. H. Hodge's scholarly book on the flora of Dominica, in which he describes the island's incredible rains: "At times the fall becomes torrential and the rivers rise suddenly to unbelievable and destructive heights, their waters churning everything before them. Dominicans describe such occurrences with the simple statement that 'the rivers had come down.' " But the rivers come down, as the Brands knew, mostly in the rainy season, mid-June to mid-January, and it was now the end of March.

True, there had been an unusual amount of rain since New Year's. Everyone I met was saying that it had been the wettest dry season they could remember. Yet the worst of the rain appeared to be over. There had been relatively little during the previous week. The most common danger from going out alone on Dominica was getting lost, and as long as I followed the Layou downstream that was no problem. I figured I could make it if I watched the weather carefully and gave myself plenty of time to scout the rapids, the only dangerous spots. And I would equip myself as well as I could against all contingencies.

Preparation is half the fun, and that night I marshaled my supplies with care. Into a sturdy canvas tote bag went the following items: an underwater mask and snorkel, a Nikonos (underwater) camera loaded with high-speed Ektachrome, a coconut (husked), a sealed plastic compass and a ball-point pen, the latter two items knotted into a red kerchief (for emergency signaling).

Among my camping supplies I found a one-pint plastic jar with a watertight lid. It was already half full of a homemade mixture of roasted oats, nuts, raisins, dates and honey, known to health-food addicts as crunchy granola. I can live on it happily for days—well, if not happily, at least healthily. On top of the granola I added two folded sheets of paper torn from a yellow legal pad; an extra cassette of film; five waterproof matches and the striker torn from their box, bound with a rubber band (the whole box would not fit); four wadded-up Eastern Caribbean dollar bills, each worth approximately 50 cents U.S. Like the bandanna, the money and matches were basically emergency stores.

To make doubly sure that I would not get lost, I located the gorge on my map and cut out that section with my Swiss Army knife. I folded the scrap of map and jammed it into the jar, which I then sealed and added to the contents of my canvas bag. I knotted the lanyard of my knife to one of the handles of the bag.

Finally, I took 50 feet of nylon parachute cord, doubled it over three times and wrapped its multiple strands tightly around the mouth of the bag. The result looked distressingly like a sackful of kittens. Ignoring the ill omen, I set my alarm for 5:30 and turned out the light.

All night it rained. Or so it seemed through fitful sleep. When I looked at the clock at 5 a.m. the stuff was still drumming on the roof. I had been drenched in plenty of Dominican downpours, but none had fallen this steadily. Damn my luck! I might be ready to go alone, but not to risk the rivers coming down. I turned off the alarm and rolled over.

At 7 o'clock I woke again and put on the shorts, sweatshirt and sneakers I had planned to wear on the river trip. I walked under dripping eaves to the porch beside the dining room and read until 8 a.m., when breakfast was served. Gray clouds piled over the mountain ridges, broke apart and raced down the slopes carrying rain. The Roseau Valley widened below me toward the sea. Rain filled it completely. Beyond, the sun shone and the sea was a dazzling blue.

At breakfast I was joined by a young American couple. Like me, they were in a low mood. The second day of rain in a row, they moaned. The second day? I was incredulous. So far as I knew, the day before had been dry. If it had rained yesterday at Island House, as my companions said, and not on Diablotin, as I knew, then perhaps the same would be the case today. I could at least drive up and see.

An hour later, driving north along the coast road, I was able to switch off my windshield wipers. I had picked up two local hitchhikers on

Trunk buttresses rising in graceful curves help stabilize a châtaignier tree that is rooted in spongy rain-forest soil.

their way to tend their provision gardens, the little patches hacked out of the forest where Dominicans raise root crops and bananas. The vegetable gardeners went up, they told me, every Sunday. I asked them what they thought of my prospects on the Layou. They looked toward mountains draped in clouds, just as I had been anxiously doing for an hour. No good, they said. But when we came to a bridge over the Layou near the point where it entered the Caribbean, the river seemed placid enough, riffling over shallows studded with dry-topped boulders that would have been underwater had the stream been in flood.

The road followed the course of the river inland for a mile or two and then crossed another bridge just below the end of the gorge. In the pool 30 feet below, the slow-moving water was so clear that we could see bottom. Crossing the bridge, we had a quick glimpse into the gorge itself as a shaft of sunlight beamed into it. Well, you could try it, they said without much conviction. But look out if the water turns muddy.

The road made a 12-mile detour around the gorge before regaining the river. I dropped off the hitchhikers and by 10 o'clock I had parked my car at the end of a spur road at Bells. I was three hours behind schedule, but I still had eight hours of daylight left, which was about as long as the trip had taken the Brands. I took my first step into the river, pursued by the yapping dogs that abound in every settlement.

For the first half mile below Bells the Layou ran wide, shallow and clear. Provision gardens lined its right bank, some protected by rough rock dikes. I soon found it was easier to walk in the water than to scramble over the mossy boulders, so I kept near the main channel.

Behind me the village disappeared around a bend. The provision gardens gave way to a thicket of brush and trees. The river margins grew narrower, the valley walls steeper. Clouds still hung heavily overhead, but it rained only once during my first hour in the river, and that a brief shower. Still, I hurried as fast as I could, not knowing what to expect ahead. By now the gorge had become completely wild and its steep sides unclimbable. It was obvious that the only way out was to continue on or to retrace my steps. I began to fret at the slow progress I was making through the water, slogging along thigh deep, forced to feel for my footing over unseen, slippery rocks.

Ahead, a little blue heron walked stiffly in the shallows. Three times it took flight as I approached, each time landing farther downstream. Luring me on? Then I lost it. A kingfisher dashed across the river. With its large head and short wings, it looked grotesque after the heron's graceful lines, almost too clumsily designed to fly at all. The rain began again. I inspected the water for any change of color. Smooth round snails the size of a fingertip studded the rocks. Little clingfish, with suckers on their bellies that permitted them to hold on to the rocks in the current, scattered as I splashed by.

As the river slued from side to side of the gradually narrowing chasm, a pattern emerged. A broad, shallow riffle, 70 yards or so across and no more than a foot or two deep, would begin to constrict. The water would deepen, and as the banks closed in, large boulders would squeeze the current into a few swift channels. Finally, veering headlong at a 45° angle toward a sheer cliff face, the river would pour over a steep ledge, ricochet off the cliff and sweep into a deep, calm pool. These pools, 15 to 20 feet deep, extended along the vertical wall of rock for 100 to 150 yards, cleaving to one side of the canyon or the other. Each pool widened and grew shallower, graduating finally to another ankle-deep riffle of small rocks and sand bars.

The best way I found to navigate these pools was to walk until the water was up to my waist, then slip my face mask over my eyes and flop forward into the stream, letting the current carry me as I kicked along the bottom. With one hand I fended my way over and past boulders; with the other, I clutched my sack. Everything that could be damaged by water was secure inside the sealed jar. Eventually the current would begin to carry me faster than I cared to go, as it squeezed between narrowing walls and larger boulders. At that point I would ease to the side and study the best passage over the lip and into the next pool. Taking a big breath, I would slip off a rock and let myself be swept through—feet first if possible, sometimes head over heels—into the pool. At the rock wall the current would make an abrupt turn and I would emerge into calm water, peering down through my face mask at large fish hanging in the shadows under the cliff.

At these moments, the canvas bag proved even more useful than I had anticipated. Turned upside down, it trapped air and served during my plunges as a life preserver. Swimming in fresh water with only one hand, and with sneakers on, was harder than I had supposed, and I was always glad when my feet finally touched bottom again and I could walk out into another riffle.

After negotiating three or four pools in this haphazard manner, I was beginning to feel pretty cocky. The worst that could happen to me now, I felt, would be to slip on the maddeningly slick rocks and break a leg. So I was especially careful crossing them. I was even beginning to wonder when the Layou would live up to its reputation as the island's largest river. I had seen New England brooks that rivaled this one.

In that frame of mind I jumped into one more raceway. Suddenly my leg slammed against a hard slimy surface and I felt my sweatshirt grabbed from below. I was snagged on a tree trunk that had jammed underwater between a rock and the cliff. The current piled and frothed over my head, and I felt for the first time the real force of the river. I do not suppose it took me more than five seconds to rip free, but it was a bad moment. My heart was pounding when I finally found myself floating in the pool beyond. I felt very much alone, and the impulse to go back seized me. But I was already too far.

After that I moved still more carefully, searching when possible for ways to climb down to the pools rather than shoot into them. This took time—more and more time—as each new stream and rivulet poured into the Layou, some plummeting down the cliffs in white ribbons, each swelling the volume of the water that was carrying me down.

Now in the deep pools I could no longer see the bottom through my mask. If not muddy, the water was at least getting disturbingly opaque. The rain was still intermittent. But what, I wondered, was taking place miles away on the upper slopes of Diablotin, the source of so much of the water flowing into the river? I had an all-too-vivid image of rain, as I had seen it in the Valley of Desolation, soaking the earth until it could absorb no more; water pouring into streams, clawing chunks of soil away from the banks, turning rivers into brown torrents.

That image might have become an obsession but for a more immediate concern. I was finding it harder each time now to find a way down into the pools without throwing myself on the mercy of the current. The valley walls were growing higher and much closer together. The boulders lining the narrow margins and constricting the current in the middle were sometimes as large as small houses. I no longer dared swim between them. And getting around or over them was becoming more a feat of mountaineering than of river running. Once I had to untie my sack and loop my parachute cord over a fallen tree to lower myself down a 20-foot drop. This took time, and I calculated that it was already early afternoon. In the gorge the light would fade early.

Then, as my feet touched bottom in yet one more pool, I looked up to discover three men in tattered clothes carrying bamboo fishing poles and walking toward me along a sand bar. They seemed even more startled than I was. And well they might be, to see a stranger in sopping sweatshirt and shorts, with a face mask and snorkel perched atop his head, a camera around his neck and a waterlogged sack in his hand.

I asked them how much farther to the bridge. Not too far, they said, but you cannot get through; the water is too high. I did not want to believe them. I must go on, I said.

Well, there is a path around the worst part; it starts there, behind that *bois canon.* The oldest of the three men pointed downstream to a small tree with large leaves, growing on a strip of river bottom where the chasm widened a bit. I saw only the same impenetrable wall of green that grew wherever the rock was not too steep. They had climbed down into the gorge to fish, he said, and they would show me the way out later, if I wished, in a couple of hours.

I said I could not wait, so they walked on up the river and I walked down. After flailing around in the underbrush for a while, I found what I took to be the path they meant and decided to try it. The faint trail climbed to a narrow setback about 50 feet above the gorge. After I had gone a short way, the sound of the river to my right grew thunderous. Leaving my bag on the trail, I carefully made my way down a little watercourse that descended like a flight of rock steps and disappeared over the cliff into the river. I worked my way to the edge and peered down. Below me the entire river, confined between rock walls, piled up behind two enormous boulders. A smooth, muscular six-foot arc of water plunged down between them to smash into a boiling froth at the bottom. I would as soon have gone over Niagara in a barrel as to consign myself willingly to that spillway. I gave silent thanks to whatever agency had sent the fishermen down to me at just that moment, for I do not see how, once into that current and hemmed in by the cliffs, I could have backed out. Either the Brands were far more courageous than I or the water was lower when they went through. Probably both.

I returned, picked up my bag, and walked an eighth of a mile farther along the track, crossing several more tributary streams. And as I walked something began to nag at my attention. Something had changed. I noticed the cheeping of a hummingbird nearby and the peeping of tree frogs. I heard the gentle splash of the stream I had just crossed, as it fell into the Layou. All at once I was aware that the dull roar of the river that had been with me from the time I started out, muting the ordinary forest sounds, had ceased. Was the river still there?

Carefully I eased myself down a steep bank below the trail, clinging to roots and branches. I kept losing my footing, but there was plenty to hang on to. Finally I slid the last few feet into the welcoming roots of a giant *châtaignier* that somehow clung to the very edge of the cliff, growing out over the chasm at a 30° angle. Between some of its buttresses the earth had been washed away and I could see down into a pool 30 feet below. The far cliff rose straight up out of the water, not more than 20 yards distant, towering hundreds of feet above the top of my *châtaignier*. The entire pool, whose ends I could not see, lay in shadow. It must have been very deep, for there was no sign of any current. The cascade that fed it was hidden around a bend, the sound of the water muffled by baffles of mossy rock. A wind rustled the leaves of a *palmiste* nearby but did not stir the water's surface. The mirror image of the blue-brown cliff, clad in ferns and bromeliads, plunged into the depths. A large fish coasted just below the surface. I hung in the roots like a child up a tree. This, surely, was the pool the Brands had described. Here lay the essence of this island of forests and rivers. And though I was not floating in it, I could at least see my reflection staring up at me out of the water, framed in the ruddy roots of the *châtaignier,* like the grinning face of the Cheshire Cat. And I was alone.

A half mile farther down, the trail rejoined the river at its juncture with a large stream. And as I emerged onto a sandbank I noticed that the sun was out in full force for the first time that day. I sat on a rock like a lizard, ate half of my crunchy granola, cracked my coconut and drank the milk from it—all but a bit that dribbled out over my chin.

I had come, I figured from my scrap of a map, about two thirds of the way from Bells to the bridge. The cliff on my right, the side Diablotin lay on, was higher than ever, but the map seemed to show that from here on the valley broadened somewhat along the left bank. I decided to plunge ahead. And indeed, whenever the river became too violent, I was able to find my way along the rocky margin of the south bank, moving slowly because the rocks were still as slippery as ice. I glided easily through several more pools, but none approached the secret grandeur of the one I had looked down on.

Then I glanced up from a pool, and ahead of me was the swinging bridge. Save for the fishermen, it was the first sign of man I had seen since starting my journey. I grabbed hold of a rock and eased myself out of the water. Above me a dog barked.

Doomsday for an Island Town

The people of St. Pierre, on the French-owned island of Martinique, had reason to count their blessings in early 1902. Life in their town—the so-called little Paris of the West Indies—was congenial and bountiful. Gaily painted stucco houses lined steep streets that led to lush green hills. Beyond them, just four miles away, loomed 4,428-foot Mont Pelée, a picturesque backdrop for the town and a favored picnic spot as well.

St. Pierre's inhabitants, mainly Creole, had long regarded Pelée as a benevolent presence. The mountain provided protection from the trade winds. Down its flanks flowed cool streams like the Blanche and the Roxelane to refresh the town. True, the mountain had been known to erupt—the area's fertile volcanic soil showed as much—but Pelée had been silent since 1851. The townsfolk did not dream that the placid mountain might again turn violent.

The mountain tried to tell them. In early April, 1902, hikers to the top reported that they had sniffed sulfurous odors coming from steam vents. By month's end a summit crater had filled with heated water—a suggestion of some subterranean rupture. Early in May Pelée began spewing black clouds of smoke; waters offshore were strewn with birds killed by the heat and poison fumes. Then the wall of the newly formed crater lake gave way. An avalanche of hot mud raced down the Rivière Blanche, obliterating a sugar mill and more than 30 workmen. But St. Pierre's officials pooh-poohed the need to evacuate the town.

On the morning of May 8 Pelée literally burst open. A fiery cloud of superheated steam and gases, laced with bits of glowing rock, enveloped St. Pierre. Within two minutes, the town was an inferno of fires, fallen buildings and burned bodies. The lethal cloud then roared out to sea.

Rescuers from a French warship who ventured ashore hours later found that of some 30,000 people in the town, only three were alive. Two soon died; the survivor was a lawbreaker named Ludger Sylbaris, who was in an underground dungeon when Pelée struck.

Sylbaris spent his later years traveling with a circus, billed as the man who had lived through Doomsday. To his testimony was added the vivid realism of photographs like those at right and on following pages, taken before and after the event—some of them sold as stereopticon slides for home viewers.

Several weeks before the catastrophe, islanders watch the smokings of Mont Pelée from a hill near the town of Gros Morne 50 miles away. At this time, despite the ominous black cloud above the volcano, Martinique's population viewed the spectacle with the curiosity of sightseers—and only the merest tinge of unease.

Several days before the eruption, a few boatloads of St. Pierre's inhabitants —mostly women and younger children dispatched by worried menfolk— flee the threatened town. To calm fears, Martinique's governor boldly took up residence there, only to perish in the fire started by the molten lava.

More than two weeks after it blew up, Mont Pelée continues to disgorge huge gushers of smoke and ash. Not until September, five months after the blast, did the volcano quiet down.

Bereft of greenery, the banks of the
Rivière Blanche show the results
of scouring by a torrent of boiling mud
mixed with boulders and tree trunks.

The Rivière Roxelane winds through
the shambles of St. Pierre's finest
residential district, incinerated by an
incandescent and poisonous cloud.

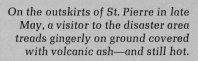

On the outskirts of St. Pierre in late
May, a visitor to the disaster area
treads gingerly on ground covered
with volcanic ash—and still hot.

72/

During the months just after the
cataclysmic outburst, St. Pierre is a
ghost town, ruined and desolate,
3,000 of its houses crumbled by
the still-smouldering Mont Pelée.
Resettlement began in 1904, but today
the population is less than a fourth
its former size. The scarred hillsides,
however, have long since recovered
their green mantle, and a tropical
wilderness flourishes once again.

3/ The Rising Blue Mountains

*And there is no sound but the swish of water in the gullies
And trees struggling in the high Jamaica winds.*

D. H. CARBERRY/ *NATURE*

The expeditionary force that Oliver Cromwell sent to the Caribbean in December 1654 to carry out his so-called Western Design had two commanders. There was an admiral, William Penn, father of the future colonizer of Pennsylvania. And there was a general, Robert Venables, former governor of the city of Liverpool. The historian Germán Arciniegas has aptly summed up their less than harmonious performance: "Penn smiled every time Venables made a blunder, and Venables made a blunder every time he gave an order or mapped a campaign."

Cromwell's Western Design—a grandiose scheme for expanding England's holdings in the Caribbean at the expense of Spain's—was itself something of a blunder. England's Lord Protector not only had picked the wrong commanders, but also had underestimated the strength of several of the Spanish garrisons. The prime candidates for attack were the islands of Puerto Rico, Hispaniola and Cuba. Then, if all went well with these operations, the next target was to be Cartagena on the northeastern coast of South America—part of the Spanish Main.

With a motley force of nearly 7,000 men, Cromwell's deputies struck first at Hispaniola. The Spanish defenders, though outnumbered, easily beat back the foe. Penn and Venables, looking desperately for some way to save their pride, picked a new target: Jamaica. It lay only a few leagues to the west and was virtually ungarrisoned.

Xaymaca, as its Arawak inhabitants called it, had been discovered by Columbus on his second voyage in 1494 and colonized by Spain in 1510. The Spaniards started plantations, but their attempts to work the cane and cotton fields with slave labor were a failure; the indigenous Arawak Indians pined, sickened and died under slavery. The Africans brought in to succeed them proved a tougher lot, but Jamaica languished nonetheless. By 1655 it had become a third-rate colony—clearly a pushover, even for Admiral Penn and General Venables.

The Spaniards offered only short-lived resistance; the African slaves did better. They melted into Jamaica's forbidding interior, ready to take on anyone who tried to pursue them. The Maroons, as they came to be known (the name probably derived from the Spanish *cimarrón*, meaning wild or unruly), traveled shadowy forest trails and rugged mountain ridges as they evaded the island's new proprietors. Mastering hit-and-run guerrilla tactics, they repeatedly humiliated English troops sent to rout them. The era of their rebellion was effectively ended by inbreeding and by the weakening of a warrior class that gradually found itself without a first-class opponent to fight.

Today, the two main havens in which the Maroons hid out are still among the wildest, most intriguing and least explored areas in the Antilles. One, the so-called Cockpit Country of north-central Jamaica *(pages 94-95)*, is a weird redundancy of deep depressions and precipitous conical hills, a pattern repeated for some 500 square miles. Viewed from a plane, it brings to mind a tangle of roller coasters, vertiginously rising and dipping as they run to all points on the horizon.

Once a level limestone plateau, the Cockpit Country is a classic variety of what earth scientists call karst topography, an extraordinarily jagged and pitted landscape formed as the porous and permeable limestone gradually succumbs to the dissolving action of rain water and underground drainage. The formerly flat surface thus became a studding of hills and cave-ridden sinkholes—the "cockpits" that gave the region its name. An undulant green carpet of vegetation covers the masses of craggy limestone, but it only serves to disguise the perils of getting about. Climbing in and out of the cockpits is particularly hazardous; the walls are so steep-sided that a secure place for the human foot is hard to locate. Nor is a climber's self-confidence helped by the sight of ominous openings in the rock here and there, hinting at the stygian passageways and chambers beneath the surface.

The Maroons were able to cope with this formidable environment because in some cockpits the bottoms were flat and surprisingly tillable —once the trees were cleared. They were also extensive enough to hold an entire settlement. The site of one former Maroon camp, Petty River Bottom, measures seven acres, and other cockpit bottoms are as large as baseball fields. Most, however, remain unexplored.

The sheer cussedness of the terrain is likely to ensure that the Cockpit Country will remain wilderness. The Jamaican government makes no effort to attract tourists to the area. As one recent guidebook to the island warned: "The going is extremely rough, and take a compass, as there will be no one to help you if you get lost."

The other major sanctuary of the Maroons was almost as frustrating to their pursuers. The Blue Mountains of southeast Jamaica, named for the haze that tints their heights, are marked by knife-edged ridges, plunging valleys and rushing streams, complicated everywhere by dense tropical forest. The mountains rise abruptly to over 7,000 feet; indeed, they are still rising—in some places at a rate of a foot every 1,000 years—because the faulting that heaved them up above the rest of the island 25 million years ago is by no means at an end.

Since the time of the Maroons, some of the mountains have yielded to the march of commerce. Plantations high on their slopes grow the beans that produce the delectable brew known as Blue Mountain coffee. But elsewhere—notably along the eastern side of the 25-mile-long range—it is still possible to savor the isolation that made the area a Maroon redoubt. There, as in the Cockpit Country, no settlements or roads exist; the only way to move about is to beat through the bush along trails made by a few hardy hunters of wild boar.

My own effort to penetrate this part of Jamaica began in the capital of Kingston with a visit to the University of the West Indies. That may seem an oddly citified route to a wilderness destination, but I had my reasons. Not only did I want to get into the mountains, but I hoped while doing so to learn something of the geologic origins of Jamaica and the entire Greater Antilles. I had yet another hope, which I was too abashed to admit openly: I wanted to be shown some tangible proof of Jamaica's great age which, as I knew from my reading, went back millions and millions of years.

I needed a traveling companion who was both knowing guide and articulate geologist. John Roobol, the faculty member to whom I was directed, filled the bill nicely. A bluff 200-pounder with muttonchop sideburns, he was obviously an outdoorsman as well as an academician. Moreover, our meeting was luckily timed. But for an exam he had scheduled for that day, a Friday, he would have been gone by then, en-

Rust-colored boulders of andesite lava, their edges rounded by tumbling in the bed of a Jamaican stream, give evidence of the island's volcanic origin. Named for the Andes Mountains, where it is also found, this andesite is tinted by oxidized iron within the rock.

camped with some fellow geologists in a remote upland valley in the very part of the Blue Mountains I wanted to see. Roobol was planning to join his colleagues the next day, and agreed to take me along.

Early on Saturday morning he picked me up at my hotel for the drive to our jumping-off place, the mountain town of Whitehall in the island's southeasternmost parish of St. Thomas. In the car with us was Mike Ashcroft, a medical doctor connected with the university and, as I was to discover, a tireless hiker. Ashcroft was going into the valley, as Edmund Hillary said of Everest, because it was there.

Roobol's motive was more pragmatic; in a sense, he was bent on a more sophisticated version of my own unannounced quest for tangible evidence of Jamaica's past. But Roobol knew exactly what he was going to look for: samples of a certain rare volcanic rock—a black variety called tachylyte. Like all volcanic rocks, tachylyte is formed when molten lava cools and hardens, but the process is so swift that the result is a natural glass. On a previous trip Roobol had found stream-worn bits of tachylyte, the first specimens discovered in Jamaica, on the gravel flats near the mouth of the Morant River, which drains part of the southern flank of the Blue Mountains. He had probed in vain upstream, looking for the mother lode, but access farther along the Morant was blocked by several waterfalls, one almost 100 feet high. This same feature, in fact, had preserved the isolation of the upland valley in which Roobol's friends were now camping.

At Whitehall we left the car and picked up two local residents, Joseph McPherson and his son Little, who were to help get us to our destination. Since our valley lay along the upper reaches of the East Arm of the Morant River, we should have been able to reach the camp by following the watercourse; but the waterfalls stood athwart the river. We had to circumvent this barrier by taking a roundabout route up one side of an eminence called Big Hill and down the other.

The start of our march took us diagonally up the west wall of a V-shaped valley above Whitehall. At first we followed a road bulldozed in the late 1960s by government foresters. As we climbed, coconut palms and mango trees poked through a low cover of shrubs and grasses. Higher up, the foresters' road disappeared; landslides had either blocked the way or wiped out whole sections of the road. All that remained were raw gashes of red earth and rock, some treacherously tending to slide away underfoot. They had to be negotiated in a headlong rush, a maneuver made more difficult by a change in the terrain; the low cover had given way to a forest of Caribbean pine.

The weather, at least, was in our favor. Though heavy rains are common in the Blue Mountains—the moisture-laden northeast trades spill most of their accumulation there—this morning was bright and sunny. The sea, about nine miles to the south, was in view through gaps in the trees; so were some of the Blue Mountain peaks. Half a dozen black dots wheeled in the air: John Crows, Ashcroft told me, the ubiquitous turkey vultures of Jamaica. A lovely sight on the wing, they are a fright close up, with their featherless, wrinkled, red heads. The original John Crow, the story goes, was a red-faced, black-cassocked English vicar who liked his rum. The islanders had found the resemblance between him and the turkey vultures irresistible.

As we traveled higher on Big Hill the track grew steeper, narrower and more overgrown with brush and bracken. We were now walking single file, our view increasingly obscured by the vegetation. Around noon we reached a small clearing where we paused and ate a quick lunch. Ashcroft's altimeter read 3,800 feet; we were just about at the top of Big Hill. From here on, our way was precipitously downward, through a forest heavily swathed in ferns, mosses and bromeliads, the graceful air plants that make their homes in trees. The exertion was beginning to take its toll on me, and my throat felt parched. Unfortunately, the streams were all lower down. Rather than carry water, Ashcroft explained, experienced hikers in Jamaica drink from the reservoirs formed by the cupped leaves of the bromeliads. To prove his point he ripped a plant off the side of one tree and poured out a couple of quarts of brown liquid. It was full of flies, mosquitoes and decaying vegetable matter, but reasonably potable for all that, he assured me, when strained through a mesh cloth. I opted to nurse my thirst.

Our descent took several more hours, some of the time along the face of slopes so steep that I could reach out and touch the mountainside. I was, in fact, grateful to be able to do so; on my other side was a drop of hundreds of feet, and a good grip on the trees and roots that protruded from the mountain prevented a possibly disastrous plunge. Lower down, the angle of the slope lessened and the forest floor became more open, the trees larger. My companions ticked off some of the names: Santa Maria; mountain guava; blue mahoe; and boarwood, a name derived from the folk belief that wounded hogs gash the bark with their tusks and rub their wounds against the sap.

After a while we could hear water flowing below us. We quickened our pace and were sweating like stevedores when at last we dropped down onto a bank of a river—the East Arm of the Morant. Crystal-clear water spilled over and around large boulders, and a deep pool absorbed shafts of brilliant sunlight. We shucked our clothes and in a moment were in the stream, drinking and swimming at the same time.

A few minutes later two of Roobol's geologist friends appeared, wading downriver toward us: Bill Horsfield, a colleague at the university, and Tony Porter, a member of the staff of the Jamaican government's Mines and Geology Division. It was Porter who had organized this expedition to further a government survey of the island's mineral resources. He and Horsfield were each carrying a rucksack of rock samples—basalt, andesite and granodiorite—some jet black, all of them sparkling. The two men had whacked the samples off boulders and outcrops upstream, using their sturdy, forged-steel geologist's hammers. The shiny rocks looked impressive to me, but I gathered that they held no surprises for their finders. These were varieties of igneous rocks —hot molten material that had cooled and solidified—and they were abundant in this part of the mountains.

Our campsite was only 100 yards downstream in a small clearing. There we met the rest of the party—several recruits from Whitehall under the stewardship of a man named Festus Davis, whom Porter had engaged to clear the trail into the valley. The campsite was canopied by a fountain-like stand of bamboo. This graceful giant of the grass family had been imported into the Caribbean from the Far East during the early colonial period because of its multiple uses, from building material to food container. The only other traces of habitation were suggested by a large breadfruit tree across the river and several Seville orange trees nearby—scraggly survivors of the farming that the Maroons had undertaken at their hideaways. They left little else to catch an anthropologist's eye. Instead of pottery, they had used bamboo and calabash gourds, and their huts were of mud and wattle.

Our particular stretch of river was a close replica of the upper reaches of the Layou on Dominica, with one difference. Here the mosquitoes were merciless, blackening arms and legs in a minute's sitting. One defense was to put on long trousers and long-sleeved shirt and smear head and hands with insect repellent. Or you could immerse yourself in the river until sundown, when, I was assured, the assault would cease. I tried both, and longed for darkness.

While in the river I watched Little McPherson and another Jamaican hunt the pools for large, clawed fresh-water shrimp, far more delicate than the salt-water crustaceans and much esteemed by the islanders, who call them crayfish. Using underwater masks to spot their quarry, the two men would grab the smaller crayfish—six inches or so—with their bare hands and toss them up onto the shore, where Festus Davis popped them into a bamboo basket. The larger crayfish, a foot or more long, with claws equally long, tended to give nasty nips to bare hands, no matter how quick; Little shot these big ones with his homemade spear gun, powered with strips of old inner tube. By evening the hunters had collected quite a batch, and Festus put a kettle on to boil.

As we ate, the light began to die and the mosquitoes stopped biting; they were, I was pleased to learn, members of a species that does its work only by day. In their place fireflies filled the shadows. These beetles were not the little capsule-shaped creatures I knew from my youth: they were the size of the end of my thumb, and instead of one light at the end of their tail, they had two where you would expect their eyes to be. They looked like tiny cars with headlights.

The day's long trek was over, the mosquitoes were gone, our stomachs were full of crayfish. The only sounds were the river, the call of mockingbirds and the peeping of tree frogs. We sat around the fire drinking coffee, at perfect peace. The time had come, I decided, for my geology lesson. When I remarked that I could imagine no better ambiance in which to hear the story of Jamaica's beginnings, neither Roobol nor Horsfield needed much urging.

They began with two caveats. One, that the story would be necessarily sketchy. Two, that I had to cooperate by letting my mind leap back over immense spans of time. There was no way I could understand Jamaica's history, Roobol explained, without first harking back to a period when there was no Jamaica, no Antilles, no Caribbean.

That was some 200 million years ago, when 70 per cent of the earth's surface was one enormous ocean and the remainder was land, massed in a single giant continent, Pangaea. (The name, compounded of the Greek words for "all earth," was bestowed on this supercontinent early in the 20th Century by a German meteorologist, Alfred Wegener.)

About 190 million years ago Pangaea started to break up into separate land masses—the continents of the future. The breakup was forced by the rise and fall of hot, viscous rock in the mantle below the earth's crust. As the land masses moved away from one another, they rode atop "plates"—sections of the earth's crust and mantle—that were some 60 miles thick and from hundreds to thousands of miles across.

The image of supercolossal plates in ponderous drift around the plan-

A pitted marble block lies in gleaming contrast to dark volcanic rocks along the Morant River in southeast Jamaica. Originally formed deep inside the earth from limestone subjected to great pressure and high temperatures, the marble was gradually uplifted over some 50 million years and eventually torn loose by the flooding river. The potholes in the marble were drilled by pebbles caught in shallow depressions in the block and swirled around by rushing waters.

et was a stupefying one, and I confessed as much. But Roobol and Horsfield assured me that geologists almost universally accept the plate theory, or, as it is formally called, the theory of plate tectonics. Its basic premise is that all of the earth's structures—mountains, volcanoes, ocean trenches, and so on—are formed over long periods by the plates' movements away from and toward each other.

It was during one collision some 140 million years ago that Jamaica and the other islands of the Greater Antilles first appeared. The so-called East Pacific-Caribbean plate moved toward and slid under the North American plate, releasing such tremendous energy that great amounts of volcanic material were formed and eventually hurled above sea level. Mixed in with this material was limestone, the compressed remains of clams, snails, protozoa and other aquatic life in the warm shallow seas around the volcanoes. The result was an arc of islands in the northern Caribbean—Jamaica and the rest of the Greater Antilles.

At this point, I observed that Jamaica's rise sounded to me like the performance of a lady in a levitation act, coming up neatly and all at once. Not so, I was told; a better analogy would be to a platoon of soldiers emerging uncertainly from their foxholes, some lurching forward, some falling back. The effect, in Jamaica's case, was to crack and fault the island like a three-dimensional jigsaw puzzle.

No sooner had Jamaica been thrust up above sea level than weathering and erosion went to work to wear it down. The island became the victim of a kind of seesawing of powerful forces. In periods when the plate below Jamaica became relatively inactive and volcanism ceased, weathering and erosion would prevail. At one time the island was so ground down that the tropical ocean poured across it, and colonies of rudists—conical clams as long as six feet—built huge reefs over the surface. At another time, some 40 million years ago, Jamaica sank until all of it was underwater and in places covered almost to a mile's depth by limestone—the raw material of today's Cockpit Country.

Renewed plate activity would periodically thrust Jamaica upwards again. Some 25 million years ago the East Pacific-Caribbean plate broke apart, and the Caribbean portion changed direction from northeast to east, causing new stresses. This brought a new era of faulting and uplift that created major structures like Blue Mountains and faults such as the 24,720-foot-deep Cayman Trough west of Jamaica. Continuing plate movement in more recent times has caused earthquakes; one of them destroyed Kingston in 1907.

The campfire was dying, the hour was late, and all of us were ready to settle down for the night. I hung my hammock between two trees and as I lay there, lulled by the ripple of the river and the muted sounds from the forest, I concluded that the geologists' story had made sense —hypothetically. But I could still not relate their account of plates 60 miles thick, drifting continents, and molten magma miles beneath the sea to the sights and sounds of this secluded valley. If only I could be shown some really compelling piece of evidence: that was my last waking thought.

The next day I followed Roobol up and down the river for miles, examining likely looking boulders and outcrops for the tachylyte he sought. He found none, nor any of the even more exotic kind of evidence I yearned for. We went back to camp, collected the other men, and headed out of the valley.

My wish was to be fulfilled, however. On the way back, where the government foresters' crumbling road sliced across the face of the valley above Whitehall, Roobol and Horsfield spotted a convoluted rock formation, several square feet in area, that looked to me like a mass of rising muffins. I had a momentary vision of cake frosting being squeezed out of a giant pastry tube, and my fancy proved not altogether farfetched. This rock, my companions explained, was pillow lava—part of the volcanic material spewed up 100 million years ago. Originally, they estimated, the pillow lava had lain at least 6,000 feet below the surface of the sea, where the enormous weight of the water at that depth had precluded the formation of the tiny gas bubbles found in most other kinds of lava. Our pillow lava had traveled quite a distance upward —more than 1,000 feet above sea level—and had only recently been uncovered in a landslide.

Far below me the Caribbean stretched away, and behind me ridge after ridge of the mountains receded into the blue mist. I reached out and touched the lava, and felt that my mission had been accomplished.

A Rock in Many Guises

PHOTOGRAPHS BY DAN BUDNIK

A brief geological biography of the island of Jamaica might read thus: Born about 140 million years ago when volcanic mountains reared up from the bottom of the northern Caribbean. Emerged from the sea laden with limestone, a rock formed by the accumulation on the ocean bottom of myriad shells of marine animals, the skeletons of coral polyps and the remains of plankton. Subsided into the sea about 100 million years later. Reappeared 20 million years ago, again thickly layered with limestone.

Though this history is measured in spans of time almost impossible for human minds to arrange in perspective, its evidences are dramatically strewn across Jamaica today in the mass of limestone that makes up fully two thirds of the island's surface. These formations range from towering blocks wrested from seaside cliffs (right) to tortuous outcroppings on the inland hills to lacy networks of underground caves. One particularly fascinating area of the interior—called the Cockpit Country—is pocked with huge limestone sinkholes (pages 94-95) overgrown with luxuriant greenery.

This extraordinary diversity of forms is due to limestone's unique combination of qualities. As rocks go, limestone is unusually soft; it is also porous. As a result it is an easy target for the forces of erosion and weathering: the buffetings of wind and waves, breakdown by plants that lodge in and expand cracks in the rock, and dissolution by the acid carried in rain water. On Jamaica this chemical assault is especially fierce because of the island's heavy rainfall—up to 150 inches a year in places—and the high temperatures that speed the acid's action.

The very fact of limestone's vulnerability provides it with a surpassing virtue: it is never monotonous to look upon. Even as it is being pounded and battered, undermined and eaten away, it takes on countless unpredictable shapes that lend remarkable variety to the landscape and create a kind of stark, abstract beauty that few sculptors could match.

To human eyes these natural structures may seem immutable, rigidly fixed in the state in which they are seen. Once in a while a major flood or earthquake will visibly transform a section of limestone. But the processes of decomposition and disintegration are slower paced. No less potent, they are unrelenting reminders of the transience of the most imposing rock masses.

Limestone blocks up to 35 feet high, torn by waves from coastal cliffs, lie in the surf on the southeastern shore of Jamaica. The gridlike pattern resembling an elephant's hide, on the foreground boulder, was produced by ancient earth shifts that fractured the rock before it rose from the sea.

The Battleground Where Land Meets Sea

The effects of the elements upon Jamaica's limestone are most nakedly exposed where land and sea meet. Here the rock receives the full brunt of the forces that shatter and pulverize it. The attacks are sometimes spectacular (*right*) and oftentimes subtle (*overleaf*), but always persistent. They have to be: it takes about 4,000 years for 12 inches of the rock to disappear from the land. Since Jamaica's limestone is 5,000 feet thick in places, it could take as much as 20 million years or more—barring major geological upheavals—to carry out nature's scheme for reducing Jamaica to fragments and recommitting it to the bottom of the sea.

The 1,600-foot-high cliff shown here, near Cutlass Point on Jamaica's south coast, offers a prime example of the all-out onslaught that may, in six million years or so, demolish the entire rock mass. Streams coursing down from the top have fluted the rock and hurricane rains have further gouged out these gullies between the ridges. Seeds have taken root, sprouted and widened the cracks in the rock. And all the while, at sea level, the surf cuts like an ax, hacking away at the cliff's base and leaving great white scars as a portent of more assaults to come.

Surf chews at the base of the cliff at Cutlass Point, inflicting slow but sure damage. With no intervening beach to blunt the sea's frontal attack, the limestone suffers steady undermining —a process hastened by storms.

Crumbling boulders, torn by storm waves from the limestone shelf in the background, edge a beach at Round Hill. Though they now stand beyond the calm sea's reach, the rocks face an added threat—breakdown by the roots of beach morning-glories.

A once-solid expanse of limestone lies in a state of decomposition and disarray. Water washing into the flat tidal area from nearby Jackson Bay filled this salt-marsh lagoon and weathered and eroded the surface of the rock into jagged remnants.

The Deceptive Embrace of Tropic Greenery

Inland from the coasts, out of range of the sea's slashing attacks, Jamaica's limestone formations take on a different look—more softly worn, more weathered. The forces that assail them here are less brutal. Often, indeed, the inland limestone seems in full accord with its surroundings, even serving on occasion as a muted backdrop to a swath of exuberant greenery (left).

Yet Jamaica's lush vegetation and ample rains contribute to limestone's downfall as inexorably as does the savage sea. One major method of attack is chemical warfare. Rain water picks up carbon dioxide as it falls through the air; as the water soaks into the ground it picks up more carbon dioxide from decomposing plants and becomes a weak solution of carbonic acid. The limestone, which is almost pure calcium carbonate, dissolves in the dilute acid.

In this process, the limestone masses contribute to their own destruction. After they have dissolved, some of the mineral residues add fertility to the soil. More plants spring up, more carbon dioxide is released when they decompose—and more limestone rock is destroyed. Thus the cycle of terrestrial decay continues, feeding on itself.

Left high and dry 100,000 years ago by a slowly receding sea, a 50-foot limestone cliff stands amid encroaching underbrush, including a yellow-flowered shrub called nightsage.

An embattled veteran near the island's north shore displays its wounds. Acidic rain water has heavily pocked the limestone's upper half; mineral residues have blackened and streaked its face; a tree has rooted in an incipient crack. The deep horizontal notch at the bottom is a souvenir of earlier times, carved out by lapping waves before the shoreline shifted.

Outcroppings of buried limestone —estimated to be 45 million years old —form a brittle, dwindling rock enclave on a fertile slope in southern Jamaica. The deep vertical gashes in the rocks are the result of weathering by moist air and ground water that has enlarged the ancient fractures.

The composition of the unseen limestone that underlies this section of the Hellshire Hills dictates the look of the landscape. The limestone bedrock is an unusually porous variety, called honeycomb, that soaks up all the rain it gets. As a result, the surface soil is left arid and thin, hospitable only to cactus and thorny scrub.

Baffling Mazes beneath the Jungle Cover

Perhaps the most astonishing change that occurs in limestone is one geologists call karstification. This formidable term refers to the impact of rainfall on a limestone area; the heavier the rainfall, the more dramatic the impact. The receptive rock sops up the rain water, which tends to drain down through the limestone's primary structural lines and joints. Over the millennia, through chemical action, the water sculpts the limestone into a labyrinth of deep sinkholes, huge caves and long underground passages.

The region of Karst in Yugoslavia gave its name to this sort of bizarre topography, which also abounds in Jamaica. Here, over a 500-square-mile wilderness in the north-central part of the island aptly called the Cockpit Country, conical hills alternate with deep depressions—some more than a half mile across and as much as 300 feet deep.

Very few of the subterranean passageways and caverns that underlie the Cockpit Country and parts of Jamaica's south coast (overleaf) have ever been explored. Yet they play a vital role in limestone's grand design, serving as conduits to collect its waterborne materials and transport them back to the sea.

The rolling Cockpit Country—so named because its sinkholes resemble the arenas in which Jamaicans staged cockfights—wears a thick mantle of trees. About five million years ago the region was a flat limestone plateau.

A slender shaft of sunlight pokes through a small collapse in the slowly dissolving dome of an ancient cave beneath the Hellshire Hills.

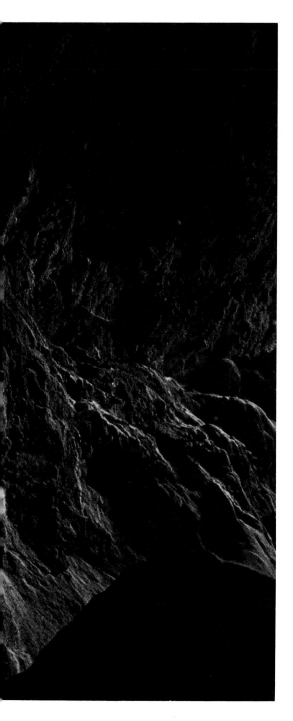

Foot-long stalactites, sculptured like graceful plant leaves, hang from a cave roof.

A cave floor is studded with stream-borne "pearls"—limestone-coated snail shells.

Reflecting the green of sun-dappled shrubbery, Cave River bursts from its underground course where a gigantic cavern has collapsed. A

short distance on, the river goes underground again,.then reappears seven miles away and relays its limestone cargo along to the sea.

4/ A Taste of Thinner Air

I saw for the first time the magnificent mountains
of the Cordillera Central spread out before my enchanted eyes.
Far above the others rose up two giants.

ERIK EKMAN/ IN SEARCH OF MONTE TINA

I am sitting sprawled at the top of a 9,000-foot mountain called El Yaque in the middle of the island of Hispaniola, cold, sick, miserable and a trifle dubious about what only yesterday seemed such an intriguing challenge: to reach the highest point in the Antilles. My misery stems in part from a depressing mixture of knowledge and uncertainty; I know that Yaque, which I have climbed to get the clearest possible view of my goal, is not the highest point. But I can only guess at which of the twin peaks barely visible about five miles away can claim the title —and I will have to climb them both to find out.

This realization reinforces the physical cause of my low spirits. The hour is just past 5 a.m. and the sun is still behind a thin layer of cirrus clouds on the horizon. The temperature is somewhere in the 40s. The tips of my fingers are numb. My head aches. My whole body feels sore. Climbing up here has tired me beyond reason. If I were anywhere else I would think I was coming down with a bad case of flu. Here, I know it is altitude sickness, the first symptom of oxygen starvation. Altitude affects some people more than others and I am one of the unlucky ones.

I knew when I set out to stand on the roof of the Antillean archipelago that the undertaking would be less of an alpine exercise than scaling Mount Everest (29,028 feet) or the Matterhorn (14,690 feet). No mountain in the Antilles compares with them or with such snow-topped tropical mountains as 19,340-foot Kilimanjaro in East Africa. But climbers who assault these more formidable rock piles at least know not only exactly how high they are, but exactly *where* they are.

I was surprised to find, when I arrived in the Caribbean on my latest trip, that hardly anybody seemed to know the location, elevation or name of the highest point in the Antilles. Some guess, logically enough, that it must be on Cuba, the biggest island. Actually, Cuba tops out at something over 6,500 feet. Jamaicans speak of their own Blue Mountains as being the supreme challenge to climbers in the Caribbean, but Jamaica's high point is 7,388-foot Blue Mountain Peak. A Haitian businessman told me that the topmost point in the Antilles lay somewhere in his country, but he couldn't say exactly where this peak might be, nor could he put a name to it.

As it turned out, my businessman informant had the right island but the wrong country. The highest point in the Antilles, I am now prepared to state, is in the Dominican Republic's portion of Hispaniola, in the Cordillera Central, the mountain chain that forms the island's backbone. For well over a century, Caribbean geographical experts have firmly believed that somewhere in the Cordillera stands a 10,000-foot mountain. But the faith that moves mountains seems to have shifted this particular peak around like the indicator on a ouija board.

The uncertainty began with the late Sir Robert H. Schomburgk, British consul in the Dominican Republic's capital, Santo Domingo, from 1848 to 1857 and a geographer of some repute. In 1851 Sir Robert scaled a peak in the Cordillera Central, estimated its height at 10,300 feet and, on the basis of his wide experience in the region, declared it to be the highest point in the Antilles. From among the several different names by which the mountain was known locally he selected Monte Tina. (The mountain has a catch basin on its summit and *tina,* in Spanish, is a large earthen tub.) Most cartographers thereafter obediently placed a 10,300-foot Monte Tina somewhere in the middle of the Cordillera.

In time, other investigators began to sound notes of doubt, or at least caution, about Schomburgk's mountain. There was some skepticism as to its real height and, because of its various names, some confusion about its exact location. Among the doubters was a priest-scientist named Miguel Fuertes. In the course of a 1912 botanical expedition into the Cordillera, Padre Fuertes came upon a mountain named La Rucilla (from the local pronunciation of *rosilla,* or reddish) perhaps because of the reddish grass that clothed its slopes. He climbed it, computed its altitude at 9,367 feet and suggested in his report that La Rucilla —not Schomburgk's Monte Tina—was the highest point in the Antilles.

Few people paid much attention to the Fuertes report. One who did was a fellow botanist, an extraordinary Swede named Erik Ekman. A brilliant scholar who spoke and wrote seven languages, Ekman came to the Antilles in 1913 as a young man and spent the rest of his life there collecting plants. He worked with incredible intensity, disappearing into the bush, afoot and alone, for months at a time, living with the local people, drying his specimens in the ovens of village bakers. Before he died at 47 in 1931 he had collected and classified more than 2,000 new plant species, a record approached by few collectors.

Ekman was always looking for remote habitats where he might discover new plants. He used to badger Dominicans about their mountains. "Which is the highest?" he would ask. They always told him what they had learned from their school geography books: "Monte Tina, 3,140 meters (10,302 feet), in the Cordillera Central." Ekman had his doubts. He had read Padre Fuertes' report: moreover, gazing northeastward from the summit of 8,773-foot Pic La Selle in Haiti, he had seen not only Fuertes' mountain but a companion peak, both taller than La Selle and neither of them anywhere near where Monte Tina was supposed to be.

Late in the summer of 1929 Ekman set out with what for him was a superbly equipped expedition—a guide and two mules—to settle the matter for himself. He found Padre Fuertes' mountain and, pushing west, he found its companion. This was a mountain massif called La Pelona (Baldy), that rises to become what Ekman described as "an extensive treeless plain . . . whose existence gives the mountain its name." From this plateau rose twin peaks, "one covered with pines with small areas of red rocks completely free of vegetation, and the other very steep and craggy, with black pointed rocks."

Ekman first climbed the pine-topped peak and read the elevation from his altimeter: 10,394 feet. Then he scaled the craggy one, only to find that he had been preceded by, of all people, the United States Marines, who had occupied the Dominican Republic from 1916 to 1924 during a period of political unrest. The Marines had installed a surveyor's brass triangulation plate, but had neglected to record the altitude. Ekman put it at 10,424 feet, making the craggy peak, in his opinion, "the highest mountain in the Dominican Republic and thus in all the Antilles." The great collector had bagged a pair of crowning peaks. And he later nailed down his discovery by ascertaining that Schomburgk's Monte Tina was only 7,220 feet high.

Ekman's estimate was good enough for Generalissimo Rafael Leonidas Trujillo Molina, the dictator who ruled the Dominican Republic from 1930 until his assassination in 1961. Among the things he named after himself was Ekman's "highest point" in the Antilles, which became, officially, Pico Trujillo. The dictator's successors have now largely erased his name from the map of the Dominican Republic. Ciudad Trujillo is again Santo Domingo and Pico Trujillo is now Pico Duarte after Juan Pablo Duarte, a 19th Century leader in the Dominicans' struggle for independence from Haiti.

But legends are harder to kill than dictators. Possibly the most authoritative text on the Caribbean is the *History of the British West Indies* by Sir Alan Burns, published in 1954. In it, Sir Alan states flatly that the highest point in the West Indies is Monte Tina, on Hispaniola, at 10,300 feet. No less mystifying, a bilingual topographical map put out by the U.S. Army Corps of Engineers, updated to 1968 and bearing all the latest and most accurate information, shows the heights of both Pico Duarte and its companion—identified as La Pelona—as exactly 3,087 meters, or 10,128 feet. Two peaks side by side and the same height down to the last meter? It seemed highly improbable. Could Ekman have been mistaken? Or the Corps of Engineers?

Now here I was on top of El Yaque, a spur of La Rucilla, the mountain Padre Fuertes had mistakenly championed as the highest point in the Antilles. The dome of La Rucilla rose behind me to the northwest. Three miles to the southwest of La Rucilla and separated from it by a deep saddle stood the double-crowned mountain I had decided to think of, to avoid confusion, as Pelona-Duarte. I could understand better now why the location of the highest point in the Antilles had remained so long in doubt. From where I sat, La Rucilla did look taller than Pelona-Duarte and the twin peaks looked as evenly matched as my map said they were. I could not tell which I would have to scale to reach the highest spot in the Antilles. But if all went well, the Great Pelona-Duarte Expedition—its members now awaiting me in the camp below—would be there by afternoon and I would settle the matter, to my satisfaction at least, once and for all.

The expedition consisted of five men and three animals—two mules and a horse, all small but tough. The men were a mixed bag. The guide, Nengo, was a tall, narrow, taciturn young man with a Charlie Chaplin mustache and an occasional fey grin. His friend Mauricio was in charge of the pack animals. Primo Iglesias, an artist, Alain Liogier, a botany professor and El Americano—as Nengo and Mauricio called me—completed the party. Alain had made the expedition possible. Dominican government officials had either ignored my questions about Pelona-Duarte or responded with genial ignorance. But during a call to the New York Botanical Garden, I had been told that Liogier, Director of Botany at the Botanical Garden in Santo Domingo, and connected with the university there, might be interested in my project. He was.

I could not have invented a better field commander than this amiable Frenchman who spoke fluent Spanish and English as well as French, and who had earned a biology degree in Havana and taught the subject at New York's Manhattan College before settling in Santo Domingo. He had never visited Pelona-Duarte and, like Ekman, was always eager to explore new plant habitats.

Alain recruited for the trip his friend Primo Iglesias, who drew illustrations for Alain's weekly newspaper articles on the Dominican flora. Primo's English equaled my Spanish, so we communicated largely with smiles and handshakes. He made a perfect executive officer to Alain's captain. His wife's family lived in Jarabacoa, our starting point, and Primo seemed to know everybody in the region. He arranged everything. He hired a Land Rover to take us on an hour's rough ride from Jarabacoa to a little end-of-the-road town called La Ciénaga; without him we would very likely not even have reached La Ciénaga. On the way, at a crossroads town called Manabao, we were stopped by the commander of a small army detachment there. Primo spent an hour wrangling with this officer for permission to go into the mountains. *Muy peligroso!* the man kept repeating, waggling a forefinger from side to side in the Latin American gesture of negation. He was explicit about what he meant by "very dangerous." Either we would be mistaken for Communist guerrillas and shot by an army patrol, he warned, or we would get washed away by the rain.

The latter seemed more likely. While we talked, the rain drummed deafeningly on the tin roof of the guard post. Within minutes the streets of Manabao were flooded a foot deep. Eventually the rain eased up and the guard commander reluctantly let us go, but even after that we lost an hour waiting at various fords for rivers to subside, and spent another hour clearing the road of a rockslide triggered by the rain. Finally we reached La Ciénaga. Waiting for us there were Nengo, Mauricio and the two-mule, one-horse pack train—all hired by Primo. He had originally ordered five mules, but I had said that seemed like too many since I felt uncomfortable on muleback and preferred to walk.

We left La Ciénaga shortly after dawn the next day under a blessedly clear sky. That day's passage carried us from La Ciénaga at 3,500

Berries of the parasitic conde de pino vine add color to the somber trunk of its pine-tree host. A kin of the mistletoe, the conde de pino—Spanish for count of the pine—may be so named because it lives off trees as nobles once lived off peasants. The vine absorbs nutrients by sending its roots into the life-giving vascular tissue of the host, seldom killing it directly but making it more susceptible to disease.

feet to the 8,700-foot main ridge of the Cordillera. For several miles we followed the left bank of the Rio Tablones, a tributary of the Rio Yaque del Norte, one of Hispaniola's major rivers. The lush tropical undergrowth was rich with orchids whose distracting beauty increased the difficulty of avoiding the deep and plentiful mudholes.

Leaving the Tablones, we turned up a relentlessly steep mule track that wound among a series of ridges. In that rain-rich country, trails not only wash out, they wash *in*. Soon we were climbing up a narrow, eroded trench whose sides rose above our heads. The footing was oozy mud or slippery red clay with occasional rocky patches. After half an hour or so the banks of the trench grew lower and the track drier. Ahead, a massive green mountainside rose like a wall 5,000 feet above us. Palms and large-leafed undergrowth gave way to pines, coarse bracken fern and the thin-stemmed, feathery-leafed *palo de cotorra,* or parrot tree. We plodded on, glad to feel the sun again.

By 11 o'clock, Alain, Primo and I had no more breath for conversation. Only Mauricio and Nengo seemed wholly unaffected by the pace we were setting in an effort to escape the rain. We remembered the downpour of the day before and none of us wanted to spend the night in a wet sleeping bag. Already mists were floating in, giving the mountainside a forbidding look. By noon the sun had disappeared.

At about 5,900 feet the vegetation changed abruptly to a jungle that Alain called the cloud forest. This is a heaven for an understory of ferns, bromeliads, orchids and a host of other epiphytic plants, as well as for the mosses and lichens that cover the trees. Pines share the habitat with tree ferns, slender manacla palms, the narrow-leafed conifer locally called *palo de cruz,* a yellow-flowering vine *(Odontadenia polyneura)* and all manner of lianas and creepers. I could not have moved two feet off the trail without borrowing one of the machetes Nengo and Mauricio carried in leather sheaths at their belts.

The mountain wall ahead disappeared as mists overtook us. We trudged on blindly over slippery clay, hemmed in by dense, dripping jungle. Now and again on a narrow ridge the vegetation would drop away dramatically on either side, but mist still obscured the view; we were not to see the sun again that day. As we climbed above the cloud forest, pines began to dominate again. About 2 p.m. we reached a saddle on the main ridge where open savanna sloped up steeply on either side of us, and for the first time in hours the way ahead of us was relatively flat. Near a marshy pasture stood a crude grass-thatched shelter called a *rancho,* used occasionally by Dominican government foresters. Here we unloaded the pack animals just before the rain fell.

Alain's altimeter put us at 7,900 feet. Looming above was the grassy knoll of El Yaque—studded with black rocks and widely spaced pines —around whose flanks the trail had wound. I determined to climb El Yaque at sunrise when, presumably, the sky would be clear and I could get my first look at Pelona-Duarte, four and a half miles away.

Later in the afternoon the rain stopped and we pitched our tents. Only I had come the whole way on foot; the others had taken turns riding our three pack animals. I felt tired but contented and still strong in the legs. I even volunteered to cook rice stew for supper. By the time it had boiled for an hour in that thin air I was feeling much more tired. The rice was still as hard as bird shot, but I wearily served it anyway. From then on Nengo pointedly took over the cooking. That night, as I sat beside a fiercely blazing campfire of resinous pine branches, a great wave of fatigue engulfed me. My body, born and bred at sea level, and now getting less oxygen than it was used to, was rebelling.

Certainly I felt no better the next morning as I sat catching my breath on the top of El Yaque. Having studied the twin peaks of Pelona-Duarte, I should have returned to camp for breakfast. Reluctant to move, I began instead to catalogue the life around me. I sat among thick, upright clumps of dry, yellowish, tough grass. *Pajon amargo*—bitter straw, the local people call it. Their mules and horses eat it grudgingly, but I found it lovely to look at, for natural pasture is rare in the tropics. It gave the mountains the peaceful, open look of an English park and softened the contours of a landscape that is all one huge, eroding core of upthrust igneous rock.

The bigger chunks, the size of small houses, poked sharp corners above the grasses and gnarled shrubs. The shrubs were few. *Palo de reina,* a ragged bush of the heather family with downy new leaves of a rusty brown, was well represented. So was another member of the heather family and relative of the blueberry, a yellow-flowered bush that Alain identified as *Hypericum.* There was a herbaceous plant Alain called *Senecio,* resembling the dusty miller that I knew from the Atlantic seashore. Mosses and lichen covered the rocks. And that was about all. Ekman, I recalled, had described El Yaque's summit as "the most desolate place in the entire Republic, a savanna with an infinitely poor vegetation, and black rocks bare as death." A poor place indeed for plant collectors, but I liked it. For the first time in the tropics I could recognize a majority of the species around me.

Animal life was even more limited. There were few visible insects. In the cloud forest the day before I had heard the unmistakable flute-like song of the mountain whistler. I had seen one woodpecker, a few hummingbirds, a little lizard and a small black land crab. The commonest animal had been the *cao*—the West Indian crow—that flew with raucous cries among the pines. Once or twice I had heard what might have been a parrot's call. Now the only creatures in sight were two-inch-long land snails banded in brown and yellow.

I was completing my inventory when I spied a bird flying below me. In the first shafts of the morning sun it looked all white, but through my field glasses the white separated into blue, green and a flash of red. It was one of the several varieties of Hispaniola parrot, dashing with quick wingstrokes over the mountain. I held it in my glasses for nearly a quarter of a minute, the only moving object in that enormous pastel world. The bird's vibrant beauty excited me tremendously. I forgot my tiredness and almost bounded down the slope into camp.

After coffee and a tin of sardines I felt better. While Mauricio and Nengo loaded the animals, Primo, Alain and I set out along the trail to La Compartición, the deep depression that separates La Rucilla from Pelona-Duarte. The hike down through open pine forest was not demanding. The temperature had risen comfortably into the 60s as the sun rose in a clear sky. Near the bottom of our descent, the trail crossed a brook, damming it and creating a small pool surrounded by a variety of wildflowers. A raspberry bush bore blossoms twice the size of those I knew; I would like to have seen the fruit. By the time we reached the stream, the sun was blazing through the trees. We were hot and drank deeply of the clear mountain water. From the pool, the track climbed again toward La Compartición, which we reached at midmorning. While the others were taking a break, I pushed on toward La Pelona. My goal was in sight and I was getting itchy.

Here are some of the notes I made on the climb:

I am feeling the altitude. The climb up this woods tipped on end is torture. My head pounds, my chest constricts. Out ahead of the others by 100 yards or so I am seized by the crazy notion that I must reach the top first. It begins as a game but turns deadly serious. Something about mountains brings on this madness. I think I hear hoof beats behind me. Then I realize the sound is my heart pounding. It is torture to go faster.

Mula, mula! I hear Mauricio driving the animals behind me. Catching up so soon? I look back. There are Mauricio and the animals, the horse in the lead with Primo up. Damn! They *are* gaining and I can't possibly go faster. Up. Up. Is the angle of the slope lessening? Yes, but the animals are going faster too. That's not my heart I hear now, it's the sound of hoofs striking rock just behind me.

We top the shoulder of the slope. More mountain ahead, more forest. I look back across La Compartición. Rucilla still looms above us. We must climb higher. I must rest. I flop down in the pine needles and close my eyes. Mauricio and Primo stop beside me long enough for Primo to smoke a cigarette. They move on up the trail. Primo has gone ahead, accepting my unspoken challenge. Mauricio and Primo disappear among the trees. OK, he wins.

I pull out my notebook and am writing these words when Nengo and Alain stagger into view. Alain is staggering because he is even more tired than I, Nengo because he has been bitten on the ankle by a spider he calls *cacata,* a kind of tarantula. His high shoe rubbed the swollen spot, so he is walking with one shoe off and one shoe on. Like my son John.

The three of us caught our breaths and began climbing again. Within 20 minutes we emerged onto an open savanna. There were the pack animals, unloaded and grazing peacefully. Primo stood smoking another cigarette. Mauricio, his head propped on one of the straw saddle bags, was sleeping under a tree. Behind this pastoral group, across a narrow strip of grass, there rose abruptly a rocky, pine-studded peak, and farther off a gentler slope slanted upward to a second summit.

Alain conferred with Nengo and then explained to me that we had reached El Vallecito, the plateau from which rose Pelona-Duarte's twin peaks. This was as far as the pack train could go. We would camp here and climb Pico Duarte that afternoon. Primo and Mauricio had not yet been to the top; the race was still on.

Fearful again of rain, we pitched our tents and then had a bite to eat before tackling Pico Duarte. Mauricio, who knew the trail, led the way. Nengo stayed in camp, sleeping off the effects of his spider bite.

From my notes again:

The way grows rockier and rockier. Mauricio falls back to guide Primo who now is well to the rear. I have the bit in my teeth and am feeling my own way up. And then, there is Mauricio, right behind me. He is obviously torn between two duties: leading the way as a

A nameless peak in the Dominican Republic's

Cordillera Central awaits its daily noontime drenching from lowering rain clouds. Scrubby pines and parrot trees frame the foreground.

guide and helping Primo. Finally nothing remains ahead of us but a huge pile of boulders "bare as death." Mauricio is leading now. But he has gone around the back of the rock pile. The climb from there is easier, he says. But I fool him—cheat him, really—for he has gone that way as a guide rather than as a contestant. I climb straight up. And then, there I am on top, a step or two ahead of Mauricio coming up the other side. A few minutes later Alain appears and then Primo. It is 1:30 and we are shrouded in mist.

A wooden cross was thrust between two great boulders painted with the names of a dozen stalwarts and the dates of their visits. Some trophy, I mused, for all that agony. But as we lay against the hard rock catching our breaths the clouds parted momentarily, and we had a glimpse out over the little savanna to Pico La Pelona and one quick distant glimpse of La Rucilla and El Yaque. Excitement rose in me. I was truly glad I came. The mist closed down again. Before descending to our camp, we checked Alain's pocket altimeter. It read 9,055 feet, well below Pico Duarte's official height of 10,128 feet, but that was without corrections for temperature and barometric pressure. For the moment, the figure was useful chiefly for comparison with a reading we would take on Pico La Pelona—tomorrow. I was too exhausted now for anything more than walking back to camp.

Next morning, after an early breakfast, Nengo, Primo, Alain and I headed for Pico La Pelona. Mauricio stayed in camp to tend the stock and prepare for our return trip. Nengo was determined, despite his spider bite, to resume his guide duties, even if it meant going barefoot, which he did for the rest of the trip. Primo and Alain seemed to be in fine shape and I felt better, too, though my head still ached.

I have called the peaks of Pelona-Duarte twins, and so they are—but fraternal, not identical twins. After Pico Duarte, the walk up La Pelona seemed only a stroll through an open, welcoming woodland of pine trees, not the sort of terrain that stirs one's competitive instincts. The grassy floor was sprinkled with pine needles, some dried and brown, others fresh and green. Hail had knocked the fresh needles off the trees during the storm that had overtaken us at Manabao. Two *caos* flitted from tree to tree above my head, raucously scolding me for trespassing. When I stood still they hopped down from branch to branch until they were barely 10 feet above me, close enough for me to see the sunlight turn their glossy feathers iridescent. Against their black bodies the sky appeared bluer than before, the trees a richer green.

Without actually being able to pinpoint the moment, I found myself on top of La Pelona. Primo, Nengo and Alain were already standing there on a rocky outcrop looking far down the long northeast slope into a small, uninhabited alluvial valley cupped between the mountains. Momentarily distracted by its beauty, I asked Alain about the valley. It was a plant-collector's paradise, he said wistfully, called El Valle. He had spent two weeks in the valley several years before, the first botanist ever to collect there. He had reaped a rich harvest, including a yellow-flowering herbaceous plant, never before described. It is now officially known as *Pavonia aurantia alain.*

I yearned to go on to Alain's little valley and beyond, to wander as Ekman had through these wild and seemingly endless mountains. But it was time now for the culminating moment of the expedition, the determination—to our satisfaction, at least—of the highest spot in the Antilles. Among the various heaps of rock on the summit of La Pelona one looked a little higher than the rest. Clambering up, we consulted Alain's altimeter. The needle stood exactly where it had yesterday on top of Pico Duarte: 9,055 feet. So apparently the Army Corps of Engineers map was right about the twin peaks. There is no single highest point. But I felt free to make my own choice. And remembering the cross and the painted rocks left by previous climbers on Pico Duarte, I chose La Pelona. This pristine pine grove high in the clouds was the end of my journey. A warm feeling of well-being and accomplishment swept over me—not in the least diminished by the reflection that of the four of us who had climbed Pico La Pelona that morning, I had been the last to reach the top.

NATURE WALK / Across Bonaire

PHOTOGRAPHS BY JOHN DOMINIS

The second largest island of the triplet known as the Dutch ABCs (Aruba, Bonaire, Curaçao) and lying about 60 miles north of the mainland of South America, Bonaire is a parched limestone platform set on an ancient core of igneous rock. Shaped like a boomerang—one tip pointing south, the other northwest—it measures 24 miles from end to end and some 18 miles across the middle. The south is flat; the north, where underlying rocks pierce the limestone, is hilly and includes Bonaire's summit, 784-foot Mount Brandaris.

Around the long shoreline, honeycombed limestone cliffs 10 to 40 feet high—the exposed remains of former reefs—are gnawed by the sea. At the base of the cliffs, living reefs, festooned with all manner of corals, sea fans and giant sponges, plunge into depths where the underwater visibility often exceeds 100 feet.

Inland, the red soil is poor and thin, the thorny vegetation is as drought resistant as any in the American Southwest; cactus and mesquite predominate. The 22 inches of rain that fall each year, mainly in November and December, quickly vanish into the limestone substructure or run off into shallow ponds. There the water evaporates, leaving deposits of salt—Bonaire's major export.

Some of these ponds spread inland for miles, and all are, in effect, bays connected to the sea through narrow breaks in the cliffs. In Papiamento dialect, the expressive local patois that draws on Portuguese, Spanish, French, African and Dutch words, the entries into the ponds are known as *bocas,* Spanish for mouths. The *bocas* are stoppered with low wave-raised dikes of coral rubble, but storms wash over them, adding salt to the ponds; evaporation keeps the salinity much higher than in the sea.

This supersalty soup teems with brine shrimp and larval brine flies, favorite foods of *Phoenicopterus ruber,* the roseate, or West Indian, flamingo—the most common of the world's four flamingo species. Bonaire, the Bahamian island of Great Inagua and the Yucatán peninsula are the last places where these once-plentiful birds still breed.

Standing over four feet tall on stilt legs with webbed feet, the flamingos can be seen feeding in Bonaire's ponds in groups of half a dozen to several hundred. They move in slow cadence, their long graceful necks weaving to and fro, to and fro, as they swish their sieve-like beaks through the shallow water and strain it for a meal of shrimp and larvae.

At sunrise one March morning, photographer John Dominis and I set out on foot to cross the northwestern end of Bonaire from its leeward to its windward shore. Moving quietly in the dimness of first light, we approached within 25 yards of a small group of flamingos that had come to

A LAND SNAIL AT POND'S EDGE

feed at the edge of the Slagbaai (Dutch for slough), the starting point of our walk. When they spotted us, the birds ambled off without any show of urgency; and then, suddenly, they took wing, just as the first rays of the sun were lighting the south face of Mount Brandaris.

Before heading for the mountain, our first destination, we wandered the shore of the Slagbaai for a while. Above the high-water mark we saw hundreds of delicately made, inch-long land snails, now found only in the ABCs and only as a fossil on Aruba. Sheep shells, the local people call them, for their white, almost fleecy look. At this time of year they were tightly sealed to

ROSEATE FLAMINGOS SKIMMING SLAGBAAI SALT POND

prevent any loss of vital moisture.

Two plants growing in the pulverized coral beside the Slagbaai caught our attention. One, a bushy affair with a spiky fruit, is fittingly called yerba stinki in Papiamento—roughly, stinkweed. The name derives from the repugnant odor given off by the plant's long, trumpet-like flowers when they bloom in the evening. Together with tomato and eggplant, yerba stinki is in the nightshade family, but its fruit is poisonous.

The other plant we saw at the Slagbaai was a miniature agave with spade-shaped, saw-toothed leaves. *Agave vivipara* belongs to the family of the century plant, so called because it supposedly flowers only once in a hundred years, then dies. Actually, the length of time a plant takes to bloom may be up to 60 years, depending on the species, the amount of rain it gets and the nature of the soil in which it grows. On Bonaire, *Agave vivipara* takes about seven years to store up the energy for its final grand gesture. Then, at a rate of almost a foot per day, it sends up a flower stalk some 20 feet tall, from whose branches miniature new plants sprout. These fall to the ground, where they may find a congenial spot and sufficient moisture to start a deep taproot. If not, the plants wither, although seeds within them may lie dormant, waiting for rain and the chance to germinate.

From the Slagbaai we followed a dry arm of the bay that led us northeast toward Pos Nobo. There were no trails up Mount Brandaris, but Pos Nobo, we had been told, was the

PRICKLY FRUIT OF YERBA STINKI

A YOUNG CENTURY PLANT

A GREEN IGUANA

place to start. We soon learned why. The tangle of cactus, mesquite, and acacia that grew on the lower slope of the mountain was all but impenetrable. But from Pos Nobo a dry stream bed led upward, its rocky course comparatively free of growth. It petered out, however, and the last few hundred yards up the mountain became an agony of thorns.

Meeting the Trade Wind

Emerging finally on a shoulder of Brandaris, we met the cool and very welcome breath of the trade wind. On this exposed ridge, cactus gave way to sparse clumps of grass. A few coccoloba and divi-divi trees survive here, bent and twisted and all pointing southwest, the prevailing direction of the trade wind. The divi-divis look especially odd; at lower levels they grow straight and tall.

The actual top of the mountain is a steep 200-foot-high pitch of lichen-covered boulders. Scrambling up these giant blocks, we startled two five-foot-long iguanas clinging to a rock with their sharp claws, sunning themselves. One scampered off, but the other held still long enough for John to take its picture. The island abounds with these rough-backed lizards, although they are avidly hunted for their tender white meat.

At the top of Brandaris we rested and drank deeply from our canteens. The bulk of the island stretched away in haze to the south, but to the northwest the vista was clear. Almost directly below us lay Plaj'i Funchi, a jewel of a beach, lapped by the calm waters of the leeward coast. The beach is actually the sea-

A WIND-BENT DIVI-DIVI TREE ATOP MOUNT BRANDARIS

ward side of a coral dike blocking a *boca*. It lies within the boundaries of Washington Park, recently created from a 5,928-acre plantation whose owners had somehow chosen to call it America; its commercial hub inevitably came to be known as Washington. The name of Plaj'i Funchi itself is more easily explicable; it is Papiamento for "beach of corn meal." Supplies from Curaçao used to be landed at this spot, and corn meal was evidently a staple.

From Plaj'i Funchi we would have access to Washington Park's network of roadways and paths, which would lead us eventually to the island's far shore. But first we had to get down the mountain to the beach. Due to the trade wind's drying effect, the windward side of Brandaris is more barren and open than the leeward side, and so the going down was easier than the going up. But once we were on the flat again the cactus thickets closed in on us.

Finally, after finding the boundary fence, we took heart and soon stumbled onto one of the park roads. From the mountaintop Plaj'i Funchi had looked only minutes away, but it was noon before we reached it. I cannot remember a dip in the ocean that felt more welcome.

Since our intention had been to travel into and across Bonaire's interior, we had not brought masks and snorkels. It hardly mattered; from the top of the cliffs that flanked the beach we could watch all manner of fish moving about in the clear water that makes Bonaire the finest diving spot in the Antilles. Closest

THE SHORE AT PLAJ'I FUNCHI

to shore were the stoplight parrotfish, so called because the males are green and the females are red. With their birdlike beaks, both parrotfish browse on the soft algae that live on coral; to get at their food they gnaw at the coral's hard exoskeleton, eating into its interior. In the process they ingest some calcium carbonate, which, when excreted, settles to the bottom as fine sand. Thus, parrotfish are every bit as responsible for the Caribbean's lovely white beaches as is the grinding action of the sea.

Other algae browsers, well adapted for life in the tidal zone, are a small red-striped snail called a four-toothed nerite and its less gaudy relative, the tessellate nerite. Both snails like to feast on a graceful alga called peacock's-tail, which we found growing on the rocks.

A Menace with Many Feet

From our cliff perch we detected yet another species of browser, farther from shore and deeper underwater: sea urchins, working in herds. Though they are a nuisance and occasionally a serious hazard to snorkelers, these nautical pincushions help preserve the beauty of the reefs. Moving slowly on hundreds of tiny feet, they scour the reefs of algae that might otherwise choke the corals. Most fish—and sensible men—try to give the urchin a wide berth, as the spines that cover its back are coated with a stinging mucus and break off in the flesh of any creature that disturbs it. To step on an urchin, or even brush against one, is to experience a painful wound.

Sitting on the beach after my swim

A STOPLIGHT PARROTFISH

PEACOCK'S-TAIL ALGAE AND SNAILS

A CLUSTER OF SPINY SEA URCHINS

I had an unsettling moment. I could have sworn that I had seen, out of the corner of my eye, an apparently derelict snail shell begin to move. A closer look revealed the hairy feelers, legs, and eye stalks of a hermit crab protruding from beneath the shell. This crab is ingeniously constructed so that it can work its soft body into the cavity of an abandoned snail shell, where it lives in snug safety, protected from marauding

A HERMIT CRAB IN A VASE SHELL

shore birds. Its larger claw serves quadruple duty as a weapon, a dining utensil, a flag to warn other crabs of danger and a neatly fitting door that seals the shell once the crab withdraws inside. When a hermit crab outgrows one shell, it goes to find another, trying on a number of them like a lady trying on hats.

By two in the afternoon, when the sun had lost a little of its strength, John and I headed inland again, this time on park trails. Our destination now was Pos'i Mangel, a spring (pos) at the foot of one of the hills halfway across the island. In this excessively dry country, springs are the equivalent of water holes in Africa. And when we reached Pos'i Mangel, a water hole is what it looked like: a basin, 60 feet across, walled in by brush. Perhaps those thickets were responsible for the latter half of Pos'i Mangel's name, which in Spanish means mangrove. In the center of the basin was a pool whose surface reminded me of Kipling's "great grey-green, greasy Limpopo River." Here, the green layer atop the water was not scum but duckweed.

Birds in a Bushy Tree

At the edge of the *pos,* a bushy mesquite tree spread its branches over the water. The tree was full of various kinds of birds. Most flew off when we appeared, but a West Indian mockingbird was back in minutes, hopping nimbly from limb to limb, nervously looking this way and that. Finally, perching on a twig just above the water, it took one careful glance around, quickly dipped its beak into the slimy water, tilted back its head and swallowed.

The doves were more timid. Several large blue doves that had flapped off noisily through the bush never returned. But a mixed covey of small brown ground doves and white-fronted doves flew back into the mesquite tree, and after a while ventured out onto the margin of the pond. Walking cautiously to the edge of the water, they drank their fill.

Two birds around the *pos* scorned the water. One was the little *blenchi verde,* the blue-tailed emerald hummingbird that manages nicely on Bonaire, taking nectar from the flow-

MOCKINGBIRDS IN MESQUITE TREE AT POS'I MANGEL

A HOVERING HUMMINGBIRD

A FEMALE YELLOW WARBLER

DOVES AT THE WATER HOLE

er clusters of the aloe plant. The aloe, an import from Africa and the Mediterranean, was introduced to Bonaire during slave-trade days because of its medicinal properties. It succeeded in the island's dry soil and has now become naturalized. When cut, its fleshy, succulent leaves exude a gooey substance that is used as a purgative. It also serves, if one can stomach its sickening odor, as an excellent balm for burns, including sunburn and the effects of fire coral, whose sting raises welts very much like a true burn.

Resting briefly in the scant shade of the mesquite, we watched a female yellow warbler (the male has a reddish patch on his head). She seemed to be more interested in insects than in the water hole. She was also evidently unafraid of us; several times she flew into the branches of the mesquite we were sitting under to take a closer look at us. People watching? Perhaps. In Papiamento this warbler is known as *para di misa* (bird of the mass), because it often nests in churches and can be seen, during mass, flitting back and forth over the celebrants.

Leaving Pos'i Mangel in the late afternoon, we struck off northeast through a cactus forest. The going would have been impossible but for a newly cut park road. We stopped at one point and looked back. Since we were on a bluff, we could see the tops of 30-foot-tall tree cacti protruding through a green canopy of spiny mesquite, acacia, shrubby low-lying crotons and an assortment of smaller cacti. It seemed incredible that creatures of any substantial size could survive in such thickets. Yet feral goats roam throughout the area in considerable numbers—although they have their problems. Once we surprised a kid and its mother browsing on acacia leaves beside the road. As they dashed off, we had a glimpse of the frightened baby goat racing through the brush with a piece of pear cactus the size of a dinner plate stuck to its flank.

So dry and thorny is the cactus

A POISONOUS PRICKLY POPPY

forest that even a flower as gentle as the poppy takes on a bristling look here. The prickly poppy, as it is called, is also, in fact, poisonous. We came upon one along the forest road. The flower was a pure and lovely yellow, the seed pods perfect cups that, when inverted, spilled out a palmful of tiny black seeds. The prickly poppy is the only variety of poppy that grows on Bonaire; it is also found in Mexico and Florida.

As we walked, we quickly learned

CACTUS CLUMPS NORTHEAST OF POS'I MANGEL

to loathe the common prickly-pear cactus. Its local name, *infrou*, translates as miss. I could not decide whether the reference was to its impertinent sting or its clinging nature. Probably both. It also has a devilish relative, *Opuntia curassavica*, that creeps along on the ground forming large patches as formidable to a man in sneakers—which, alas, is how I was shod—as a bed of glowing coals.

Flights of Green Screechers

Several times earlier in the day we had witnessed the furious flights of brilliant green parakeets, screeching like banshees. I knew they were parakeets because of something I had learned—and versified—from *Birds of the West Indies*, the indispensable guide by ornithologist James Bond:

Parrots squawk *(waak-waak)*,
Parakeets screech *(creek-creek)*,
Parrotlets chatter softly.

Now, as we pushed on, a small flock of screechers landed for a moment in a tree cactus, and we had a chance to confirm my identification. The parakeets of the Dutch ABCs are particularly interesting because they vary from island to island. Although all are of the same species, on Aruba they have olive-green heads; heads of yellow on Curaçao; and orange on Bonaire. But they have one habit in common: all of them dig their own deep nests inside live termite nests, apparently without disturbing the termites.

As we came nearer to Bonaire's windward shore the land grew more and more rocky and the soil thinner. We noticed our first melon cactus,

A PRICKLY-PEAR CACTUS

A PAIR OF PARAKEETS ATOP A CACTUS

A SPROUTING MELON CACTUS

the only cactus growing this near the coast, on a bare limestone terrace as flat and as hot as a blacktop parking lot. This plant enjoys certain advantages over most of its relatives in the cactus family. It presents a low profile to storm winds that play havoc with taller, more loose-jointed species, and it can endure months-long droughts without shrinking visibly. Part of its secret is that it sends taproots through cracks in limestone that may reach down 30 feet to the water table. Because of the plant's squat, round form, it offers a minimum of surface area to the drying effects of sun and wind, and this helps it resist evaporation better than most other cacti.

Despite this extensive root system, however, the melon cactus develops very slowly. A plant as big as a man's head may well be 20 years old or more. And the plant produces its fruit in a rather surreptitious fashion. First, small pinkish flowers appear amongst the cushions of stiff hairs that cover the plant. In time the flowers turn to fruits of a deep crimson, but these remain hidden like jewels among the hairs. Only as they swell and ripen do they emerge. And they are deliciously sweet.

With Bonaire's windward coast in view at last, we were again panting for a swim in the sea. But the water lay at the base of a 20-foot cliff and was anything but the placid sea we had enjoyed at Plaj'i Funchi. A steady barrage of waves pounded the rocky ramparts. We could have leaped in, but there would have been no return to shore. On this windy

A FUZZY CHITON

side of the island, most of the *bocas* act like funnels into which great seas roar, then just as tumultuously retreat, making them extremely dangerous for swimmers.

A short walk up the windward coast, we found a lower wall of rock and a *boca* more receptive to the relentlessly incoming waves— Boca Cocolishi. Here the waves spill into and through the opening to fill a protected pool behind it. At the back of the pool the incoming waters have deposited a perfect miniature beach of fine, powdery sand. We judged the center of the pool to be about six feet deep. It was filled with silvery palometa fish, a species of pompano. Every half minute or so, a fresh wash of sea water gushed in, making a foam of bubbles. This was a pool fit for kings—or, more appropriately, two very hot and tired hikers.

Lying face up in the water, we inspected our surroundings. The sides of the pool were undercut walls of ancient coral debris on which were plastered, at the splash zone, mollusks as old in design as any species of animal living on earth today. Called fuzzy chitons, they are two to three inches long and their oval shells are fashioned in eight inter-locking sections. If one is hungry enough, a stout jackknife serves to pry the chitons off the rocks. They are not bad, raw.

As we paddled about, we watched periwinkles and nerites browsing on algae in the wash and proving the value of their ability to cling. We also had a close look at the exposed remains of a now-dead brain coral, the foundations on which Bonaire's reefs are built.

Later, in a shallow depression on a rock shelf above the pool, we found a glowing mass of salt crystals lit by the fading light of a setting sun. Earlier in the day, the sun had dried this product of errant waves. When night fell, however, enough sea spray would reach the depression to dissolve the crystals again. In the morning the process would start all over again. Such is the unremitting handiwork of the sea as it goes about shaping and reshaping this fascinating island.

NERITE SNAILS ON BRAIN CORAL

CRYSTALS OF SEA SALT

SUNSET AT SURF-SPLASHED BOCA COCOLISHI

5/ In the Spirit of Crusoe

Some said it was an island no one had ever seen
and perhaps one that had just been created;
but the captain and pilot maintained
that it had to be the small Island of the Birds.   PÈRE LABAT/ 1724

Since breakfast we have been looking for Isla de Aves—the island of birds. Nothing breaks the perfect circle of the horizon. Horizon is too soft, too sibilant a word. Some guttural Anglo-Saxon sound is needed to mark the hard edge between this velvet-soft, pale-blue vault above and the foam-flecked, deep-blue sea surface, spread as if with a palette knife from way out there directly to my feet.

My feet, while I was scribbling those lines, were planted on the fore-deck of the 72-foot ketch *Alianora*. All night the upright, red-jacketed figurehead of the mythical Prince Alianora of Bessarabia, bolted to the ship's prow, had gazed steadfastly 10° west of south. Moving easily through a calm sea, *Alianora* barely heeled to the trade wind wafting over her port quarter. We were in no hurry. It was useless to search for Aves with the rising sun glaring off the water.

Aves is the devil to spot at any time of day because it is so small, so low and so far from any other seamark. It is the only exposed portion of the Aves Swell, a submarine ridge some 250 miles long and 65 miles wide that rises abruptly 9,000 feet from the sea floor and runs along a north-south line like a bowstring to the arc of the Lesser Antilles. On maps, the island of Aves appears, if at all, as a lone pinprick 140 miles west of Dominica and 350 miles north of Venezuela, the country that has held sovereignty over the island since 1865. Even a pinprick on a map exaggerates the size of Aves. It is not much longer than a half dozen city blocks and not much wider, at its widest point, than one block. Its highest elevation is nine feet above sea level. One need step only a few yards inland from any of its beaches to have an unobstructed view of the whole island.

Over the centuries Aves has been shrinking, due to the erosion of winds and waves or the subsidence of the Aves Swell or both. In another couple of centuries it may have vanished altogether. Certainly it is a lot smaller today than it was in 1705, when the observant Dominican priest, Père Labat, spent 21 days there after a sudden storm had blown his ship far off course as he traveled from Martinique to Guadeloupe. The island he described was nearly seven miles in circumference and about 50 feet high, with two satellite islets lying to the west and northwest.

Aves not only was bigger in those days, it also had trees. Labat, who tended to view the natural world through his stomach, noticed guava, wild soursop and custard-apple trees. Salt ponds and marshes supported a large population of flamingos—tasty birds when young, according to the good father. He shipped two to France. Though there were no springs or streams whatsoever, Labat noted that potable water was to be found "by digging in the sand 100 or 150 paces from the shore."

There are no trees on Aves today, and no brush, swamps or flamingos. The trees and brush have died, the swamps have dried up or have been inundated by the sea, and the flamingos have retreated to sanctuaries like Bonaire (pages 112-123), where they are safe from such gourmands as Père Labat. But though Aves is a true desert island, it is by no means a dead one. It teems with life, especially sea birds. Three quarters of a million noddies and sooty terns live there, and the offshore sea life is as untouched as any in the Caribbean. Even in 1705, Labat was astonished by the quantities and size of fish around Aves. He spoke with special wonder of a "10-foot sea serpent"—probably a moray eel.

Currently the island's most intriguing creature is an occasional but faithful visitor, the green turtle, the only one of the Caribbean's four genera of sea turtles to nest on Aves. From late July to mid-September, these 300-pound reptiles congregate in the waters off Aves to mate; at night the females climb the beaches to lay their eggs. In a sense, it was the green turtle as much as the trade wind that drove Alianora on. Besides Captain Michael Tate and two crew members, she carried six passengers who planned to spend a month on Aves studying this increasingly rare creature, much of whose life is still a mystery. I had come along to help with tagging the turtles and also to act out a long-savored fantasy: living on a desert island, though in this case not alone. As Robinson Crusoe had his Friday, I had Bill and Sue Rainey, Jack and Cindy Egan, Roy Sexton and Paul Kramer.

Bill Rainey, who headed the group, is a marine biologist with half a dozen years of field work in and around the Caribbean. He has an easy way with adjectives like benthic, for bottom-feeding fish, and nouns like berm, meaning the slanting strip of beach between the water and the flat. This was his sixth visit to Aves and the third time he had spent a month or more there. The previous summer Jack Egan had spent six bachelor weeks on Aves with the Raineys; this time he was returning with his bride, Cindy, whom he had married just three days before *Alianora* set sail in mid-July from St. Thomas in the Virgin Islands. For Cindy as for Roy and Paul, two young recruits from the Explorers Club of America, and for me, this would be our first view of Aves, and we quartered the horizon eagerly.

At 9 a.m., after Captain Tate had shot the sun and computed our position, *Alianora* changed course to due east, using the diesel to drive her into the wind. Half an hour later there was still no sight of land —only the "flaming lazulite" of the Caribbean, as Lafcadio Hearn had felicitously described it in one of his journals. The sea was dabbed with floating fronds of golden-brown lacy sargasso weed and broken now and again by sprays of flying fish, shooting out of waves and curving off on the wind in breathtaking glides.

Ten o'clock and still no sighting. We began to share some of the frustrations of boatmen from the islands to windward who still set out for Aves to take turtles for meat and to steal the eggs of both birds and turtles; turtle eggs are popular among West Indians as a remedy for impotence. Venezuela declared Aves a faunal reserve in 1972, but short of placing a full-time guard there, the edict is unenforceable. The island's obscurity remains as always its best defense. Skippers of inter-island schooners, relying on dead reckoning and eyeball navigation, have spent fruitless days in search of Aves. Twice in 1972 boats equipped with modern navigational aids went out to pick up Rainey and his party and returned without them.

Captain Tate was luckier, more adept or both. Just after 10:30, the mate, who had spent the last hour in the rigging with binoculars, sang out, "Land ho!" And there it was, a narrow yellow ribbon between sea and sky two points off the starboard bow. Within half an hour I could see a smooth green mantle spread above a golden beach with white

At a busy colony on Bonaire, roseate flamingos divide parental duties, some brooding single eggs in mud nests, others standing guard.

breakers crashing at either end. But Aves still looked tiny in that immensity of sea. Above it hung a gray haze of sea birds. Some of them, dusky brown with dove-gray caps, flew close alongside, hovering at a level with our heads. They stared at us with penetrating black eyes, made darker still by a fine line of white beneath. They were noddies, Rainey said, close relatives of the sooty terns with whom they make up 99 per cent of the island's bird population.

"You can smell it now," said the mate with a touch of malicious amusement, as Captain Tate anchored in the broad bay in the island's lee. He was right. Downwind, Aves smelled like a zoo and, though it had seemed so quiet from afar, sounded like Times Square on New Year's Eve. Once ashore, we almost had to shout to be heard over the screeching of birds and the roar of breakers on the windward shore.

All afternoon we shuttled from ship to shore in an inflated rubber dinghy, lugging our gear through the sea surge and up the steep beach. By 4:30 everything was stacked in a disorderly pile above the berm and *Alianora* was weighing anchor for St. Thomas. Only then did I get my first really good look at the island.

What remains of Aves is shaped like a footprint in the sand, a lady's right foot, triple A and high arched. The big toe points due north and is a wide, flat expanse of loose sand, pitted like a battlefield by nesting turtles. The ball of the foot is a wasteland of guano-impregnated sand covered by nesting birds, about one to every two square feet. Over the heel of the foot grows a bright green carpet of *Sesuvium portulacastrum*, the reef banana, with here and there a competing patch of *Portulaca oleracea*. Both are dense, ground-hugging creepers of the purslane family that also share a common name: survival weed. A shipwrecked sailor could chew out of their fleshy, succulent leaves a brackish liquid slightly less salty than the sea. How long he could survive on it is problematic. So perhaps the name by which the two plants are known pertains simply to the fact they are the only vegetation visible above the tide line.

A narrow, steep-sided sand bar connects the ball of the foot to the heel. At the instep one can easily flip a rock underhanded from one side of the island to the other. Storm waves and high tides sometimes wash entirely over this bar, though the normal wave action carrying in sand from the shallows tends to build it up. Here, as on the north end, the sand is deeply pocked with turtle pits.

The density of nesting birds south of the instep is lower than in the main rookery, and the springy mat of survival weed is largely intact, giving this end of the island the look of a golf course. At the very base of the heel lies a smaller replica of the northernmost expanse of sand.

To walk around the entire shoreline of Aves takes only about half an hour. All along the windward side, the surf breaks on a coral reef built on the tumbled foundations of Labat's larger island. At the north and south tips, crosscurrents and convergent waves chop the sea into a froth. In the lee of the island the water lies calm, almost glassy close to shore, surging gently against the steep crescent beach. The sandy bottom shelves off gradually, leaving the sea pale blue for a half mile.

Rainey and company made camp just south of the ball of the foot. This put them at the island's highest point, as far as possible above the threat of flooding seas, and in a good central location for the nightly turtle patrols. I went south to the heel and, in the spirit of Crusoe, pitched my solitary tent on the farthest margin of the survival weed. My tent flap opened to the rising sun and to the surf and the wind that came right off the sea, untainted by the heavy acrid scent of guano that pervaded the rest of the island. Even after I had learned every nook and mood of Aves, I was never tempted to move my tent.

Every detail of the campsite is vivid in retrospect. Let me show you around my home as it looked after a couple of weeks *in situ,* as Rainey might say of specimens found at their original locations:

I am quite alone here; the greenery to the north of me cuts off 30° of the horizon, so that I cannot see the main camp. My tent is of the latest design, its exterior now tastefully decorated with liberal white stipplings of bird droppings. A light blue tent fly serves as a roof, keeping the interior cool by day and dry when it rains. The tent itself has two windows and a door fitted with zippers and mosquito netting. The netting is firmly tied back; there are no mosquitoes or other bothersome insects on Aves save for a bird tick that occasionally bites but does not burrow under the skin.

My tent pegs are three-foot-long iron rods. When the wind blows, as the Raineys have learned, nothing less will hold in the loose sand. My tent may be an anomaly in this setting, but it is a cozy place at night or during a squall. My books, papers and camera equipment would not last long without it, for here on Aves we are only a few feet above sea level. Out on the edge of the reef, no more than 35 yards from my door, the sea is constantly bursting in a barrage of white spume. A fine salt mist covers whatever is left out overnight; sunglasses and camera lenses cloud up in minutes.

My front porch is a beachcomber's triumph. It is a wooden freight platform—freight handlers call it a pallet—that must have fallen off a passing ship. I found it nudging the island's central sand bar and towed it here through the shallows inside the reef with a length of rope I also found on the beach. All the other wood hereabout—for instance, the bamboo in the structure I have built and am now sitting under with my poncho rigged as an awning, the table under it (the seat from a rowboat) and the chairs (two mismatched packing crates)—I found and lashed onto the pallet on my way home from the sand bar. Like Robinson Crusoe after one of his salvage operations, I was towing quite a bargeload by the time I reached my landing.

An astonishing amount of flotsam reaches the minuscule shores of Aves. Last season Rainey scoured a 10-meter stretch of windward beach and found the seeds of West Indian almond, manchineel, hog plum, mango and some 50 other kinds of plants. Most of the nuts could apparently still germinate, despite their saltwater immersion. On my own beach there are probably seeds that floated past me while I was descending the Layou River in Dominica four months ago. The hog plum on the table there might be one of them. The goose barnacles on it are a sure indication that it has been afloat for several months. Countless coconuts have also washed ashore. A shipwrecked man could live for some time on their milk and meat. At the moment I have no need for such sustenance, as my supply of granola and tinned milk is plentiful, but I do eat them from bowls made of the coconut shells.

No wonder so many mainland plants, arriving as ocean-borne freight, grow on oceanic islands like the Antilles—and would still grow here, too, if Aves had not been whittled down to a tiny sandspit unable to support anything but survival weed. But if bottles could reproduce, we would be knee deep in them. They dot the beach like turtle pits. I have found no messages in them yet, but they have their uses. One of them, inverted in a wide-mouthed jar sunk in the sand, is my still. I stuff the bottle with survival weed in the morning and let the sun work on it. By nightfall the bottom of the jar holds a mouthful of water considerably less salty than the weed itself.

Of course, I am only experimenting; we have brought ample water to drink. For other needs, there is plenty of running water rolling in over the rocks out there. You could not work up much of a lather in it, but I have not used a piece of soap since I arrived—either on my dishes or my person—and I have never felt cleaner. A towel? The wind dries you in minutes even if the sun is behind a cloud. And the temperature—I suppose it is somewhere in the 80s—is just right for bare skin. Heat is no problem. My awning mitigates the sun's rays during the middle of the day. The wind is a fine air conditioner. I crawl into my tent at night, and if the wind is stronger than usual, I zip up the door and complacently recall my tortured night in a hammock on Barbuda. One could hardly imagine a softer natural bed than survival weed.

The sun divides my day. That straight piece of bamboo stuck in the sand is my clock. Now, at midday, its southward-pointing shadow is a mere stub; in mid-August, a few weeks hence, with the sun directly overhead at noon, it will cast no shadow at all. Time then to start looking for hurricanes. When one threatened last year the Raineys had to be evacuated by a Coast Guard helicopter sent from Puerto Rico. But the storm passed well south of Aves and they were back within a week.

That broken bit of conch shell a few feet to the west of my bamboo stick marks 8 a.m. The gorgonian coral the same distance to the east indicates 4 p.m. At 6 p.m. the shadow reaches a piece of elkhorn coral I have set down and I wander up the beach to help cook dinner and have a sip of warm rum. Crusoe never had it so good. We eat early because showing lights at night would scare away turtles coming in to lay. I usually take my other meals, which do not require a fire, at my tent. The others on the expedition have been splendid about respecting my privacy.

The elkhorn, by the way, was my second choice as a suppertime marker. The first one, a well-weathered whelk shell, got up and walked off, like the hedgehog croquet balls in *Alice in Wonderland*. The shell harbored a hermit crab, one of the island's corps of scavengers. Drop an orange peel or any crumb and these crabs will be on it in minutes —even in daylight, though they feed mostly at night. When the sea washes up a dead fish or a rotting piece of fruit you may find 20 or 30 assorted moving shells congregated around it, jockeying for position.

The sky is marvelously clear. For the past week a thin haze has hung in the air, but the weather broke dramatically yesterday when a line squall passed over. After a gaudy sunrise, the sky to the east-southeast grew dark. The wind rose to near gale force and the temperature dropped suddenly. Clouds closed in and a gray wall marched steadily closer, streaks of rain slanting down from a low ceiling to the choppy sea. Then it was on us—large, cold, wide-apart drops. I could see no more than 50 or 60 yards out into the bay, where the gray-green swells stood out in bold relief against the neutral backdrop of rain.

In the rain, I took my first fresh-water shower in two weeks, and afterwards I could actually pull a comb through my hair. Then, almost as abruptly as it had come, the rain quit. In minutes the sun was flickering through disintegrating clouds. The sky was washed clean.

I spend a lot of time staring across the strip of sand in front of my tent at the surf, at the sea and the sky. The view is so pure, so simple, that, as in a Mondrian painting, form and color are reduced to absolutes. Mostly I look south over the tip of the island where the sandspit rounds off and a rocky shelf begins. It is strewn with slab-sided boulders, some the size of hencoops. This is beach rock—very young in geological time—which solidified when coral rubble and sand were cemented together in layers by chemical action. As the island emerged from the sea during the last million years, the rock was exposed, undercut and broken by the surf. Slabs of the rock were tossed about, a testament to the sea's power. When the surf is high, waves clash over these rocks at nearly right angles, sending up 30-foot plumes of dazzling white spray. It is a fitting show for land's end: nothing but sea between here and the coast of Venezuela 350 miles away.

That the Venezuelans should own Aves seemed odd to the 19th Century Dutch settlers of the island of Saba, which was much nearer than Venezuela—only 125 miles away. So the Dutch claimed Aves, contending that it had once been connected to Saba. They bolstered this dubious geological assertion with the quite factual claim that Sabans went regularly to Aves to hunt for turtles and gather birds' eggs. In 1865 the Queen of Spain, asked to arbitrate the dispute, found in favor of Venezuela on the grounds that "all the islands of the Caribbean Sea were discovered by Spaniards" and that Venezuela "succeeded Spain in all its rights to the island."

Aves had been coveted by its claimants chiefly as a source of guano, and the few West Indian skippers clever enough to find the place mined all the guano they could load. Aves became smaller and lower on the horizon, a shrinkage no doubt hastened by the removal of guano. But finding the island became increasingly remunerative because of another resource, the green turtle, as the general Antillean population of these creatures rapidly diminished.

Turtles, like such other reptiles as snakes, crocodiles and lizards, are creatures of the Mesozoic era and have survived, very little changed, for 175 million years. So long a time in the cutthroat evolutionary arena implies that their food source has remained intact and that they have reproduced faster than predators could eat them. The adult green turtle feeds primarily on the ribbon-like weed called turtle grass that chokes submarine pastures in most of the shallow waters of the Caribbean. No food problem there. Moreover, until men reached the islands, mature turtles, huge and armored, were all but invulnerable.

The young, however, are virtually defenseless. Like most reptiles, sea turtles lay eggs on land and then abandon the nest. The eggs and the hatchlings, whenever and wherever they appear in the Caribbean, are the prey of a multitude of enemies, including raccoons, birds, crabs, predatory fish and even, along the coast of Central America, wild dogs. But each female green turtle lays several hundred eggs the size of Ping-Pong balls every nesting season. The eggs usually come in three to five batches of 100 to 150 each; enough eggs and hatchlings survive to maintain the species.

Or so it was until man appeared. The aboriginal Indians took many turtles but made no more impression on the vast aquatic herds than did the plains Indians on the buffalo. Modern man proved more efficient. Turtles offered an abundant supply of a fairly scarce commodity: fresh meat. Furthermore, when turned on its back and kept in the shade, a turtle could be kept alive for weeks if a bucket of sea water were splashed over it every few hours. The green turtle, named for the color of the calipee—the cartilage lining of the lower shell—was not only the most numerous of the sea turtles but also the tastiest.

As a further inducement to turtle hunters, European society developed a craving for green-turtle soup made from the calipee. Millions of green turtles were slaughtered during the 18th and 19th centuries to supply Europe's more elegant kitchens. Most calipee hunters left the rest of the turtle for the crabs. Turtle hunting required no gun, net, trap or particular skill—only patience. Hunters waited for a female to crawl up out of the sea at night onto some sandy shore to lay her eggs. Two men could flip a 300-pound green turtle on her back, taking care to dodge the powerful swipes of her long front flippers. Overturned, the huge reptile is helpless.

Members of our expedition to Aves use the same method to tag the turtles, except that we let the turtle lay her clutch of eggs before disturbing her. When the females first come up onto the beach they are very timid. They are quite nearsighted on land but can distinguish motion and light, either of which sends them in ponderous panic back to the surf. As they begin digging their nests, however, they grow less wary. Indeed, the process seems both strenuous and absorbing. When a nesting turtle lurches up the beach, she looks for a spot she likes.

Then, with her flippers, she digs a pit 9 to 18 inches deep, heaving sheets of sand out behind. When she has worked her way down to damp sand, she begins carefully scooping out an egg chamber, using her rear flippers. Once the turtles start laying, they become so entranced that one could set off rockets without disturbing them.

At this point we creep up behind the animal. One of us reaches into the nest and counts the eggs as they drop. We take out a few, weigh them and later put them back in the nest. The turtle finishes laying, covers the nest and starts back to the sea. We flip her over, saw notches into the trailing edge of her shell according to a coded numbering system and leave her until morning, when we come back and weigh her with a block and tackle attached to a tripod. Then we rivet a metal tag —the sort used to tag cattle—to the rear edge of her right-front flipper. We measure and right her. Within minutes she has regained the sea.

The numbered, self-addressed metal tag promises a reward of five dollars to anyone returning it to the University of Florida. A returned tag almost invariably means that the turtle has been butchered, but it gives Rainey some idea of where the turtles go after they leave Aves.

At one time turtles of one species or another visited nearly every sandy beach in the Antilles. No longer. Turtles, like salmon, tend to return to their birthplaces to reproduce—or so most evidence indicates. Every turtle taken, every egg destroyed when a female is captured before she can lay or when a nest is dug up, is lost to that beach forever. Nor are turtles born on other beaches likely to fill the gap. This is why Aves is covered with turtle pits, while other Antillean beaches, apparently just as attractive for nesting—but also more accessible to turtle hunters —are quite barren.

The number of pits on Aves reflects not only the relatively large turtle population, but the fact that a turtle may need more than one site to lay a single clutch of eggs. If the turtle's digging collapses the sides of the egg chamber, as often happens, she simply moves to a new site and starts digging again. One night I watched a huge old dame do this five times before giving up and going back to the sea without laying her eggs. An obstruction like a piece of driftwood also can frustrate nesting turtles, but they are incredibly persistent. If we spot one that has not laid and is headed back to sea, we can turn her, weigh her, tag her and send her off, confident that she will return the next night.

When a turtle finally has succeeded in laying, and her well-covered nest remains undisturbed, the hatchlings will appear some 60 days lat-

A ghost crab's deadly claw stops a two-inch-long, three-quarter-ounce baby turtle as the tiny prey makes a desperate dash to the sea from the sand nest where it was hatched. The burrow-dwelling crab, whose pale color and swift movement make it an efficient beach predator, will drag the struggling turtle to shelter by the back of the neck, then devour it alive.

er. They use a horny projection on the tip of the snout to break through the leathery shell. As each baby hatches in the dark subterranean nest, it wriggles out of its shell, then lies quietly until the rest of the brood is likewise ready. During this period it absorbs the remainder of the egg's yolk sac, giving it enough energy for two weeks of active swimming without eating.

When most of the 100 or more newborn babies in the batch are ready, some unknown signal inspires those on top to start pulling down the ceiling of the egg chamber, while those below work the falling sand down to the bottom. In this way the whole clutch moves up together. If the sand near the surface feels warm, indicating that the sun is shining, they stop and wait for the cool of night when their chances of evading predators are greater. Then the whole team suddenly bursts out onto the beach. No more stealth now. Though each little turtle is on its own, survival for all of them depends on swamping their predators by sheer presence of numbers.

Sensing the direction of the water by some mysterious means that seems to depend largely on sight, the hatchlings, not much bigger than elongated silver dollars, race toward the sea, while gulls and crabs hover and rush about trying to grab all they can. On Aves the major villain is the ghost crab, perfectly camouflaged to match the sand, even to tiny specks of pink and brown on its shell. With viciously sharp claws the crab grabs a hatchling by the head and tries to put out its eyes. One morning I found a sad little carcass, already partly dried by the sun, with only its eyes gone; a ghost crab must have attacked it and then been scared off. Blinded baby turtles, unable to find the sea, are helpless. Then the crabs, only slightly larger than the hatchlings themselves, can finish them off at their leisure.

Hatchlings that get to the sea swim furiously along the surface, straightaway from the island. The deeper the water they reach, the more likely they are to escape lurking jacks, barracuda or sharks. Those that reach deep water vanish from human ken for at least a year. The best guess is that they are in some remote part of the Sargasso Sea in the Atlantic above the equator, hiding among the weeds for which the Sargasso is famous, and feeding on microscopic zooplankton. Curiously, by the time they reach their yearling size of four to eight pounds, they have switched to a diet of turtle grass and they remain vegetarians for the rest of their lives.

Nobody knows how long it takes turtles to reach sexual maturity. The lightest nesting female we tagged on Aves weighed 227 pounds, but how many years she took to reach that weight is anyone's guess; there is no known way of gauging the age of turtles that have not been hatched and raised in captivity. All we know for sure—verified by the inspection of tags—is that a green turtle who has once nested on Aves will head back there again two or three years later from wherever she happens to be, homing in precisely on this dot in the sea.

I used to sit for hours on my pallet porch thinking about turtles and other such matters. I had no radio and I did not read much because we did not use lights at night; in the daytime there were better things to do. At first I worried that I was losing touch with the real world. And then I worried that I was worrying. What was wrong with losing myself in this place and pondering mysteries 30 million years old?

Gradually I relaxed and expanded, like a hermit crab coming out of its shell—in my case, shucking off the modern city into which I had fitted my existence. And as I made wider contact with my surroundings and understood more and more about the rhythmic pace of life pursued by the turtles and crabs and other creatures, I became infused with a sweet lassitude. I ate when I got hungry. I showered when it rained. My beard grew and I turned very brown all over.

Days quickly lost their identity as parts of the week. I governed my movements by the strength of the wind, the passage of squalls on the horizon, the phases of the moon. But as calendar time became blurred, the natural features of the island grew increasingly more distinct. No longer did I confuse the birds. I could tell a sooty tern or a noddy by its cry as it flew over my tent, or by the way it flapped its wings. Airborne or not, each animal observed on Aves became a composite personality, with patterns as real to me as those of friends in my city life.

Even the sky and the earth took on new meaning. I recall one night watching the moon set. The time was around midnight. The stars grew brighter. The Big Dipper dominated the northern sky. And as I had been taught in childhood, I followed its lip to the North Star. The night wore on; the Dipper tipped and finally sank behind dark clouds. For the first time in my life I experienced the purely kinetic sense—as opposed to the intellectual knowledge—that the earth was pivoting on the polestar and that I was swinging with it through the heavens.

A Teeming Underwater Realm

PHOTOGRAPHS BY RON AND VALERIE TAYLOR

Beneath the placid surface of Caribbean waters close to shore lies a teeming world of plant and animal life that rivals the variety of life on land in these tropic climes. Underwater, as above, there are forests and fields, deserts and plains, mountains and caves, providing both shelter and food for the myriad creatures living in a warm sea.

The animals thriving in this lush world are as varied as their habitats. The longlure frogfish, for example, has a modified spine on its head that it waggles as bait to tempt other species. The blue tang bears a defensive yellow dagger near its tail. And these are only two of the evolved adaptations of physical form and behavior that enliven the deadly game of survival in these waters.

Some animals—most snails, for example, and all barnacles—develop shells as tough as armor plate. Despite its fierce-sounding name, the fighting conch, in addition to wearing a shell, wiggles into the sand, shell and all, to avoid trouble. Some sea urchins bear a coat of brittle, stinging spines to nettle any potential enemy. And many fish have developed unusually brilliant colors and vivid patterns that disguise their profiles, warn predators of the bear-

ers' unpleasant taste, or that mimic the background tones and textures, blending into near invisibility.

Perhaps the most intriguing of all Caribbean creatures is coral, the wonderfully productive little polyp that can create underwater structures as massive as a walled medieval town. Protected by a tough outer skeleton, the coral is basically a colonial animal that can multiply itself into huge reefs. It also exists singly and in many different shapes; the photographs at right and on pages 150-155 show only a few. And though coral nurtures stinging cells that protect it against some predators, it is perennially gnawed away by certain snails and fish, surviving by its ability to repair itself and at the same time providing both habitat and food for other fauna.

Like so much of the Caribbean's marine life, coral flourishes close to the surface. There, warmed by the bountiful sun to a temperature that varies between 70° and 80° F., and free of the muddy effluents that darken northern coasts, the Caribbean's clear waters expose the submerged gardens to a long and fruitful growing season for the algae and other plants that form the base of the food chain in this fertile world.

A rich profusion of corals crowd the sloping face of a reef in the blue-green waters off St. John in the Virgin Islands. Like a mountainside, a reef is divided into life zones that harbor distinct animals and plants, depending on such factors as depth, sunlight, the temperature of the water and wave action. In this 25-foot-deep section, elkhorn coral dominates the top, while fire coral and sea whips pervade the steep slope, and massive, rocklike brain coral resides at the bottom.

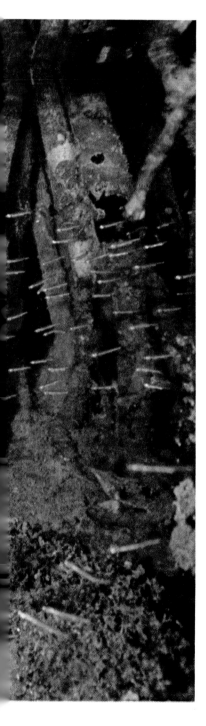

Mangrove Shallows Rooted in the Sea

In the watery margin between land and sea along leeward coasts, and in lagoons and bays, broadly rooted mangrove trees provide a unique environment for shallow-water species. Originally land plants, mangroves manage to flourish with their roots submerged in salt water—the only tree able to do so.

In order to anchor themselves firmly in the soft, sandy bottom of the intertidal zone, they send down their slender, arching stilt-roots from trunk and limbs in circumferential patterns. In this woody tangle beneath the water's surface, a compost of decayed matter—fallen leaves, seaweed, bits of dead fish—supports a garden of plants and microorganisms that in turn protects and feeds a community of small creatures. Juvenile fish such as those of the dwarf-herring species spend much of their early lives among mangrove roots, out of the heavy surf, shielded by the root maze that keeps out large predators. When these fry have grown to maturity, many of them migrate to the open seas. Other creatures—sea squirts, sponges, barnacles and oysters—cling to the roots for most of their lives. Encrusting the mangrove stilts, they feed by simply filtering and absorbing the abundant free-floating plankton within reach.

Encrusted with patches of algae, oysters, barnacles and a large, red fire sponge, mangrove roots provide a habitat for a school of dwarf herring and several crawling sea urchins.

Rough limas, like scallops, trap food with wavy tentacles.

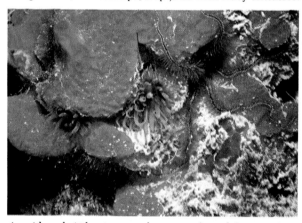

A spidery brittle star crawls over soft, red fire sponges.

A red-banded coral shrimp defensively waves its pincers.

Maritime Life in the Grassy Plains

The sandy floor of the Caribbean, like the American West, is strewn with grasslands whose denizens behave remarkably like those of any prairie. The Caribbean ghost shrimp, for example, burrows much as the prairie dog does; and small fish, like field mice, seek cover and sustenance among the grasses.

The most abundant of the grasses on this undersea plain is turtle grass *(right)*; like buffalo grass on land, it is named for its once-persistent grazer. A broad-leafed plant, turtle grass flowers in a curious lily-like form, and it reproduces by sending its pollen off on the currents as land plants use the wind.

Often mixed with turtle grass is manatee grass, which also roots and propagates in much the way land grasses do. It is named for a primary grazer, the manatee, or sea cow. As with many land animals, maritime vegetarians may sometimes overgraze a grass bed. The most common offender is the unlikely sea urchin, which travels in herds, greedily nibbling blades and stems, often so close to the roots that the grass cover dies off. Then, however, on the patches of bare sand or mud, pioneering algae may spring up and in time the grasses may return.

Searching for food, a carnivorous starfish prowls across a dense stand of mixed sea grasses, mostly turtle grass with some narrow-leafed manatee grass. In the background, mushroom-like clusters of algae thrust upward.

A longlure frogfish entices prey by moving the pinkish spine atop its head.

Black sea urchins and silvery grunts graze in a patchy turtle-grass field.

Cratered mounds in a thinly vegetated sand flat are the burrow

A fringed filefish mimics green, spotted algae.

A West Indian fighting conch nestles in the sand.

entrances dug out by ghost shrimp.

Its back camouflaged like the sea floor, a shortnose batfish prowls its hunting ground on armlike fins.

Dark Sanctuary
of the Caves

Caves and cubbyholes pocket the undersea world as they do the limestone land surfaces of the Caribbean islands. Some caves are eroded out of the submerged faces of rocky shores. Others are tunnels cut by wave action. Still others are mere crevices in coral reefs. All share certain characteristics: because they admit little light, they foster much less vegetation than do the open areas; their walls provide an anchorage for clinging species—sponges and corals, sea squirts, algae—and they offer extra protection from predators to many smaller fish.

Despite the paucity of plant food in the darkness of a cave, its fish population may be large and varied, consisting of nomads simply wandering through, individuals ducking in for safety and nocturnal feeders, like the glasseye snapper and spotted drum, which spend their days hiding inside but venture forth to hunt after dark.

These latter species, which live more or less permanently in caves, are often brightly colored and boldly patterned. No one knows why. But when exposed to the underwater photographer's flash—as in the portrait gallery on the following pages —they make a dazzling display.

*A turbulent breaking wave boils away
from the sheltering mouth of a cave.
In the bright and roiling world outside,
elkhorn and fire coral flourish
and black sea urchins graze on algae.*

Ready to puff itself up if danger strikes, a balloonfish hugs the bottom.

Flushed from a hideout by the flash camera, a spotted drum scoots off.

A red-spotted graysby bares the prickly teeth of its lower jaw.

A wary rock beauty emerges from its nook.

A blue tang searches the bottom for algae.

An angelfish nibbles red and orange sponges.

An orange-spotted filefish swims away, the spearlike file atop its head threateningly erect.

Jaws agape defensively, a glasseye snapper pauses in its search for shrimp, crab or small fish.

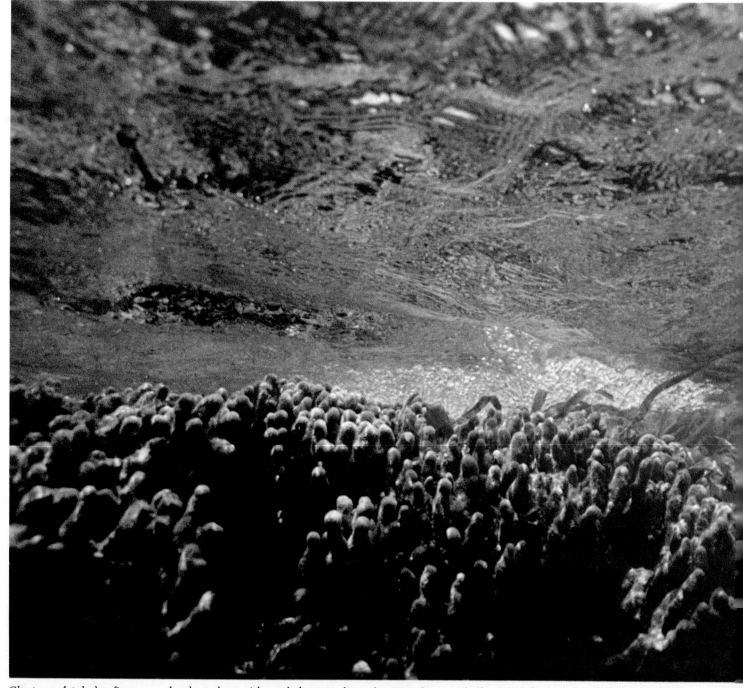

Clusters of tubular finger coral, adapted to withstand the pounding of waves, form a shallow reef flat two feet beneath the surface.

A bristle worm, marine cousin of the earthworm, feeds on coral.

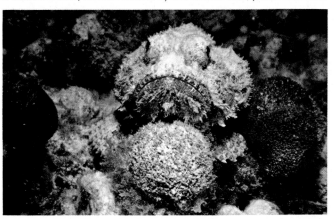

A camouflaged scorpion fish lurks hungrily amid coral rubble.

A long-armed brittle star clings to coral nubs in the wave wash.

The Coral Reef: Animal, Vegetable and Mineral

The most complex and variable community of organisms in the sea is the coral reef, composed of a group of animals, their stony skeletons and special plants.

The animal, the coral polyp, is a simple, soft-bodied organism shaped like a bag, closed at one end and with a ringlet of tentacles at its mouth to gather food. Living within its tissues are the plants, single-celled algae that coexist symbiotically with the polyp, aiding in the production of calcium carbonate that the polyp deposits around itself as a protective shell. This skeleton, which the polyp builds as it grows, takes many forms, each adapted to a location in the sea. On the sea floor are the massive brain corals and the delicate, branching sea fans and feathers. Nearer the surface are the stubby finger and elkhorn corals, able to survive without breaking because their form permits waves to flow by.

Various corals grow together to make different kinds of reefs—flats, patch reefs or the so-called gorgonian gardens where soft corals predominate. In these picturesque habitats, a host of creatures ply their trades; some come to escape predators or to cling for security in the surf, others feed on the algae and polyps, killing them. But even in death, coral contributes to Caribbean life: its skeleton, cemented by the chalky secretions of multicelled algae, becomes limestone—the building block of tropic islands.

Soft and hard corals mingle in a variegated patch reef. In the group at center is boulder-like brain coral surrounded by the furry rods and

An older male blueheaded wrasse and his yellow school feed in fire coral.

fingery projections of species of soft coral called sea whips.

Spires of cathedral coral dwarf two-inch-long blue chromises and wrasses.

Whether living or dead, the corals of a
gorgonian garden—named for their
resemblance to the trio of snake-haired
Greek goddesses—are among the
most beautiful formations in the sea.
Above is a sea fan that has been
smothered and killed by yellowish
fire coral. At near right is a bright-blue
sea fan, growing among sea whips
and feathery sea plumes 40 feet
down on the bottom of the Caribbean.

6/ Venturing beneath the Sea

If there is magic on this planet, it is contained in water.

LOREN EISELEY/ *THE IMMENSE JOURNEY*

About four miles off the south coast of St. Thomas in the Virgin Islands, a slender pinnacle of rock juts up 183 feet from the sea somewhat like the stern of a sinking ship offering a farewell salute. On nautical charts this remarkable eminence goes by the name of Frenchcap Cay, and it commands a good deal of respectful interest from passing boats. I saw it from the deck of the ketch *Alianora* on the way back from the turtle-tagging expedition to the island of Aves, and since our course was close under the lee of Frenchcap Cay, I was able to study it in some detail and more than casually.

Some dry grasses and scrub acacia had found foothold in the shadowed crevices of its near-vertical sides; barrel cactus and organ cactus appeared around the top. But the main face the cay presented to *Alianora* that morning was bare, weathered rock. Two tropicbirds with elongated streamer tails wove white traceries across the beige cliff. The rock offered just the sort of inaccessible aerie they and other sea birds choose to fish from and nest in; that was evident from the splashes of guano on its ledges. Surveying the scene, I concluded that birds —no doubt in company with lizards, crabs and insects—accounted for the faunal life on Frenchcap.

But almost at once I had second thoughts. I realized that I had been considering only half the rock—the exposed half. The chart that *Alianora's* captain had before him in the wheelhouse showed that

Frenchcap Cay rose steeply through 25 fathoms of water. Along the entire length of its submerged slope, as invisible to me as the floor of a rain forest to a man in a plane, the rock undoubtedly bristled with living things. Even within the abrasive wave zone just below the surface, every crack and cranny was certain to be harboring small corals, sponges, sea urchins, anemones, snails, chitons, algae, worms and countless other clingers. Ten feet farther down a diver would be hard pressed to find a single inch of rock surface that had not been seized upon by some animal or plant. And in close association with the rock-bound community, the sea around Frenchcap would be swarming with a population of brightly colored and fantastically shaped fish, with large fish preying on the first group and still larger fish preying on the predators.

As I speculated on this rich array of tropical marine life, typical of the waters around so many other islands and outcroppings in the Caribbean, I felt a strong urge to explore—as I always do when confronted with a new environment. At the same time I tensed a little at the thought of what might lurk in those surging waters; since Frenchcap Cay has no protective reef around it, it offers easy access to the biggest and most dangerous fish in the Caribbean.

Fear and fascination have been my twin reactions to the underwater world since I first viewed it through a face mask some 20 years ago off Diamond Head in Hawaii. The fascination is easy to explain: an almost automatic response akin to what a blind man might feel if given the gift of sight. And indeed, human eyes, when underwater, define little more than a hopeless blur. However, if a pocket of air is placed in front of them—which is what a face mask does—vision is restored and in fact magnified by 25 per cent. With the simple addition of a J-shaped snorkel tube, which allows one to breathe while face down on the surface, and rubber flippers for the feet to make swimming as effortless as walking, an incredible natural world becomes readily accessible. Seen through this looking glass, the sights are more wonderful than any that Lewis Carroll imagined.

The fright is harder to explain. It lies beyond the level of reason. Fear of the unknown is only part of it. There is also the fear of an alien element, mixed with the caution all creatures must exercise in the savage sea if they are to survive. Whenever I conjure up a single image to summarize the feeling, it invariably takes the cold, sinister form of a giant shark. I have, on occasion, seen real sharks. I have even suffered the not uncommon experience among spearfishermen of having sharks snatch away my catch, which I have always given up with no more than a whimper. But those experiences have been over in a flash. The fright I am talking about is internal, curled in the gloomy corners of my imagination, ever present as I swim.

And so, as *Alianora* sailed past Frenchcap and I learned from a member of the crew that spearfishermen in these waters had recently been troubled by sharks, my disappointment was tempered with relief. I contented myself with the memory of the other times I had snorkeled in the warm, limpid Caribbean, finding more to marvel at—and tremble at—than anywhere else I have been.

My introduction to these waters was on a winter vacation with friends, cruising in the Grenadines south of St. Vincent in the Lesser Antilles. We brought in our chartered sloop at the Tobago Cays, which lie behind one of the most extensive and lovely coral reefs in the Antilles. Anchored in a wide lagoon with a tiny islet off our stern, we spent two days exploring the shallows on the shoreward side of the reef and the tricky passes through it into deeper water. The coral maze seemed endless, the quantities of reef fish seemingly inexhaustible. There were the usual swarms of parrotfish, doctorfish, triggerfish and grunts. But I could find no spiny lobsters, which I knew ought to abound there. Nor did I see any large reef fish such as the grouper, which often allows swimmers to approach quite close. I had culinary designs on both these delicacies, I must confess, and toward that end I was carrying an eight-foot-long hand spear.

We soon found out why there was such a paucity of game. Though the cays are uninhabited, they provide a temporary base for fishermen from the nearby island of Bequia. Visiting their camp, we learned that these men did not fish from the surface in the manner of their fathers, with wicker traps or hooks and lines. Their tools were for underwater hunting and fully up-to-date: face masks, snorkels, flippers, spear guns and wire nooses to snare lobsters. Spurred by the hearty appetites of tourists and the burgeoning traffic of cruising parties, they had already cleared the long reef of lobsters, groupers and other large fish. Now they had taken to hunting miles out at sea over bottoms that ranged in depth from 6 to 12 fathoms.

The following day I went out with one of the fishermen's boats, a sturdy, hand-built dory with an outboard motor. After we had run for nearly an hour to the northeast of the cays, we stopped in seven fathoms of water. Two of the three men aboard stripped, adjusted their gear and slipped over the side. The other man stayed in the boat, using the oars to maintain his position just above them. For a while I swam on the surface, watching through a face mask.

The divers were the epitome of athletic grace. Two kicks took them down to 20 feet for a better look at the coral-encrusted bottom, which from the surface appeared flat. Spotting the waving feelers of a lobster or a promising cave formation where a lobster might be hiding, they needed only one or two more strokes of their powerful legs to send them down to 40 feet. With a quick motion they would snare their quarry with a wire noose, pull it, flapping madly, into the open and snake to the surface in a cocoon of rising bubbles.

Eventually I worked my own way to the bottom and found it was not flat at all, but a creased and cracked plateau bristling with boulder-like brain coral and elkhorn coral as tall as a man. The place swarmed with the same reef fish I had examined in shallower water off the cays. Occasionally a larger fish appeared. The ones that most interested the divers were the groupers and the equally edible hinds, both of them big enough to make the hunt worthwhile. Stalked from the surface, these fish would wind their way through the canyons and around coral outcrops to seek safety in some protected niche—an evasive tactic that for millions of years had proved effective. Now it was their undoing. I watched as one of the divers surfaced, took a cocked spear gun from the boat and descended again. His head and most of his body disappeared under a ledge. Then followed the thump of the spear gun being discharged, a flurry and a few moments of tugging to hoist a 20- to 30-pound grouper free from its hiding place. When the diver brought his catch to the surface, impaled on his spear, I rose with him.

As if on cue, there appeared out of the blue haze a half dozen four-foot blacktip sharks, obviously attracted by the death throes of the speared grouper. We looked around for the boat and found it had drifted a good quarter mile away. The diver waved to the boat and as it moved toward us we started swimming toward it. Perhaps we were in no real danger—we were, after all, bigger than the sharks—but it was an uncomfortable few minutes before we climbed aboard the dory.

I have always remembered that day not so much because of the sharks but because of the powerful sense I had of witnessing the collapse of an ancient natural balance. I had been in a place where no man had ever been, when a predator appeared who was more cunning and in some ways better equipped than the sea's hungriest creature. Fortunately, reef fish are quick to learn; wherever men have entered the sea with spears, the survivors vanish thereafter every time swimmers appear. But the place is no longer the same: it is no wonder that the pioneer French aquanaut Jacques Yves Cousteau has warned us that our grandchildren may never know what an unspoiled coral reef looks like —just as they have been denied the thrill of seeing the Western plains dark to the horizon with bison.

Many localities in the Caribbean have outlawed spearfishing entirely. It is no longer permitted, for example, in the waters off Virgin Islands National Park on St. John, or anywhere along the coasts of the Dutch island of Bonaire, which is considered the finest diving spot in the Antilles. Three years after the local government's edict against spearfishing, I went snorkeling off a number of Bonaire's beaches. It was obvious to me that the fish were less skittish than I had ever seen in waters frequented by divers. Swimming without a spear, I too felt more at ease. The air of predation that weapon gave me was gone, and with it the sense that something might, in turn, be after me.

The experience at Bonaire began even before I entered the water. From the top of the low coral cliffs that photographer John Dominis and I had walked along at Plaj'i Funchi (pages 116-117) a few days earlier, I looked out over a tide-washed limestone terrace 20 to 50 feet wide. It was a tangle of elkhorn and antler corals whose tips protruded just above the water. Among the branches, vivid orange squirrelfish, blue and green and yellow wrasses, multicolored juveniles of many species as well as other small fish took refuge like rabbits in a bramble patch. There was no way a swimmer could cross this barrier into deeper water except where the *bocas,* or mouths, made natural passes.

One day I went there to swim, taking mask and flippers. I entered the water off the little sand beach, feeling my way carefully. The water was so clear that I was able to get an unusually good look at the tiny, transparent floating animals known as zooplankton. I had known, of course, that the sea teemed with them and with invisible floating plants called phytoplankton; I had seen photographs of them in books, looking like the star- and string-shaped creatures one would expect to view only under a microscope. Now, when I focused on the water just outside my face mask, I could see little forms, like minute jellyfish, pulsing and flailing. They were about the size of snowflakes and as varied in form, some representing adult creatures and others merely the early growth stages of larger organisms such as barnacles.

I could have floated for hours watching the zooplankton, but the rest of the underwater scenery was no less entrancing. The coral thicket

A lemon shark—so called for its color—goes on the prowl. The striped pilotfish that precedes it and the remoras atop its back are two of the few species that seem safe from its predations. One of the most aggressive of marine carnivores—up to 11 feet long when mature—the lemon shark will eat sea turtles, seals and may even attack other sharks.

dropped 10 feet to a sandy bottom strewn with upthrust coral heads and patch reefs, swarming with fish that darted into their protecting shelter when I drew too close. Between the outcrops, less skittish parrotfish browsed on algae and coral. Schools of surgeonfish went by, their high-set eyes giving them a down-the-nose professorial look. The largest fish were the three-foot-long, deep-blue midnight parrotfish, which browse on coral in groups. When approached they took off, often leaving behind a white spray of excreted coral. A school of 20 small barracuda sped in from deeper water to look me over. I felt a fleeting sense of panic as they came at me in the swift rush for which their species is famous; I thought of the authenticated cases of swimmers losing a hand or a leg to a barracuda's cleaver-like bite, sometimes simply because of the tempting flash of a ring or watch or other shiny object. But these barracuda were mere youngsters—the biggest just about 18 inches long—and intent on no harm whatever. Almost all of the fish around me, in fact, seemed totally unconcerned with their new swimming companion—an ungainly apparition with a soft pink body and a large cyclopic eye, paddling across the surface spouting water from a tube.

The only positive reaction I got was from three small squid, their prominent black eyes looking enormous in frail, translucent bodies. They measured about 15 inches long—a convenient size for a reef species, though some deep-ocean squid mature to a length of 60 feet. The squid, along with its cousin, the octopus, is relatively advanced for an invertebrate, with a well-developed nervous system and an intelligence higher than all other marine animals except mammals. The trio I met seemed quite at ease playing tag with me. They would allow me to approach just so near while they maneuvered in close formation, vibrating their tail fins and changing colors from pink to brown to mottled black to almost transparent turquoise. But if I came an inch too close, they would eject water out of their body cavities through a siphon and jet away backwards, their tentacles trailing behind. Then they would stop abruptly and sidle toward me again. It was plain they felt no serious alarm at my presence; otherwise, they would have squirted a cloud of inky liquid at me, both to distract me and to conceal themselves.

Some 200 yards out from shore the jewel-like bay deepened to 30 feet. At this level, sea fans and tendrils of gorgonian coral swayed in the surge. Massive brain coral rose at intervals, alternating with more delicate formations. Jewelfish, angelfish, hinds, groupers and a hundred other species glided and turned. The shelf ended abruptly in a vertical plunge of 180 feet down to another sandy shelf. This kind of underwater drop-off is a feature of many coral reefs and presents the sea's most spectacular scenery. The cliffs are so rich visually that one is compelled to sample them piecemeal. Dive down to examine a hollow sponge, shaped like a vase big enough to accommodate Ali Baba, and you are likely to discover that beside it floats a four-foot Nassau grouper, beautifully disguised with alternating pale tan and cream-colored bands. A nearby cluster of antler coral is suddenly alive with jewelfish, their electric blue spots pinpointing a jet black ground. From a crevice at the base of the sponge protrude the menacing, wrinkled jaws of a moray eel. As in a picture puzzle of a forest scene in which the animals are camouflaged, the more one looks the more one sees.

Each day on Bonaire I practiced diving deeper and deeper, measuring my progress with a plumb line. One morning, over the drop-off at Funchi, I kicked down to about 60 feet and then let myself glide gradually upward, savoring the scenery as I went. I did this twice and was starting up a third time when a shadow passed over me. I looked up to see the largest form by many times that I had ever encountered in the sea. It was perhaps 20 feet above me and just slightly to one side. From the tip of its blunt head to its enormous tail, swinging in a slow arc to and fro, it easily surpassed 20 feet.

It was a shark.

No words can begin to reflect my own first instantaneous stab of fear. Within a second or two, however, something clicked in my memory. As I watched the behemoth move on along the edge of the drop-off and stay on a level with me as I rose, I noted its yellow spots and large, fluked tail—identical to pictures I had seen. It was a whale shark, the largest fish in the sea—and, despite its size and fearsome relatives, a gentle creature, harmless to man.

I knew from my reading that skin divers have actually climbed aboard whale sharks without the fish so much as changing course. The reporter in me said to do likewise, the coward said to get the hell out of the water. I like to think that I compromised. I swam after the big fish and got close enough to take a single shot with my underwater camera —which, like most of my underwater photographs, turned out to be sadly out of focus. But it shows enough to prove that I was there, and it does not take much urging for me to show it to friends. That single frame, however, finished my roll of film and also my determination to be brave. The whale shark moved on majestically, and I went ashore.

There was one particular underwater activity in the Caribbean that was, for me, all fascination and no fear: watching turtles mate. I witnessed this memorable spectacle more than once in the waters off the island of Aves. Because Aves has no inshore protective shelf, it is visited by more deepwater species than other places in the Antilles. And because virtually no one fishes there, the jack, barracuda, parrotfish and chub run bigger than elsewhere. But no other creatures I saw while probing offshore could match the mating turtles.

The late poet Ogden Nash once wrote: "The turtle lives 'twixt plated decks/Which practically conceal its sex./I think it clever of the turtle/In such a fix to be so fertile."

Nice lines, but misleading, according to my observations at Aves. Not cleverness but persistence makes turtles fertile. The mating process, from the time the male roughly places his slightly concave, lower shell atop the female's rounded back until the time he releases her, has been observed to last more than nine hours and may go on intermittently over a period of several days. Nash was also wrong in saying the sex of turtles is concealed. In the case of green sea turtles, at any rate, it is apparent at a glance. The male has a much longer tail, approximately two and a half feet for a 300-pound male versus half that for a comparably sized female.

The male uses his tail as one of three clamps with which he fastens himself to the female, curving it around and under the base of her shell. Each of the male's front flippers is armed with a thick, blunt thumb claw, which he hooks over the forward edge of the female's shell. With his own flippers thus immobilized in this awkward hug, the male rides about piggyback at the whim of his mate.

Sailors and turtle hunters have long noted this behavior, since the pair must come to the surface every few minutes for air. There they are particularly conspicuous because the female, fighting the weight of the huge male, flails the water in an effort to get her own head high enough to breathe. Sometimes the pair remains splashing about for minutes at a time. At almost any hour of the day or night during the July and August mating season off Aves, one can spot several mating pairs cavorting on the surface. From such a vantage, the coupling appears to be more a prolonged battle than a tender act.

Seen from underwater—an opportunity few human observers have had—the actions of the turtles seem more lyrical. Snorkeling in the bay near my campsite, I could regularly expect to encounter several mating pairs. If there was any contention, it was started by numerous unattached males. Often these bachelors would approach me, obviously bent on amour. At 20 feet or so they would suddenly realize that they had made a terrible mistake; veering off, they would swim away with swift strokes. These aggressive stags, sometimes as many as five in number, pestered the mating pairs, badgering the performing swain by nipping at the vulnerable trailing edges of his immobile flippers. All he could do to defend himself was crane his neck around and try to bite back. Whereas green turtles are quite pacific toward human beings and never even tried to bite a hand when, on land, our turtle taggers were taking measurements of their heads, here in the water they gave nasty nips to each other with their sharp beaks. I saw one male turtle so ravaged along the flippers that bones actually protruded from his flesh.

The sequel to the turtles' watery coupling is played out on land, sometime later and at night. During the dark hours the fertilized females pull themselves laboriously up the beach, as they have done for millions upon millions of years, to hide their clutches of eggs. Night after night on Aves we monitored these arrivals until our vigils became as routine as if we had been spending the hours on guard duty.

One night, however, was different from all others. I had been on the late shift, and around two in the morning I returned to my tent. But I was not sleepy and decided to sit outside for a bit. After a few minutes I saw in the shifting moonlight a dark shape moving in the choppy water about 20 yards away. Though by now the sight of female turtles coming up the beach was familiar to me, I had never seen one make the entire passage from the water onto the sand to begin the ritual of egg laying. Few people have. The slightest movement or light usually scares off a female that is making up her mind to come ashore. Now, as I watched, the dark form moved closer to the beach. Moonlight glinted off her wet shell. She stranded in the wash, shifting in and out with each wave, then turned her body toward land and raised her head on a long neck to peer directly at my tent. I held my breath. That turn of head, that large staring eye, that square-cut beak outlined against the foam-mottled ocean—the family resemblance to dinosaurs was unmistakable. I might have been watching the emergence of the first reptile from the primeval sea.

On she came now, heaving her great bulk forward out of the surf three or four strokes at a time, then resting. I could see her gulping, and I knew that but for the sound of the surf I would have heard the sharp, hissing intake of air, almost a sigh, bolstering the legend that turtles cry. Their eyes do drip tears, but they are the product of glands by which sea turtles, like many other marine animals, excrete excess salt.

My turtle had now reached the top of the berm, and she began to dig a body pit. I waited a few minutes and then made a large circle behind my tent and down to the water's edge so that I could approach her from behind. By the time I came near she had begun the agonizingly delicate operation of hollowing out an egg chamber in the loose sand.

While I waited to count the clutch of eggs that would follow, I rolled on my back, lying against the slant of the berm with my bare feet in the wash. Out of the corner of my eye I saw another form in the surf, a dark shape moving steadily against the flow of the waves. Another female turtle, no doubt. But this time I saw the oncoming form as a symbol of all the creatures beneath the sea. The back of my neck tingled. I felt reptilian eyes boring into me. And who knew what other cold, impassive eyes? Moonlight that a moment before had seemed warm and romantic turned somehow somber.

Near me a prehistoric creature was performing a ritual older than the Blue Mountains of Jamaica. In front of me surged the waves and counterwaves, currents and countercurrents of the implacable sea from which life itself arose. Perhaps, after all, the fear that I felt in the sea was only awe. Suddenly and simultaneously I was back at the summit of La Pelona, in the cave on Barbuda, in the Layou River gorge and on Peter Island under another moon. I knew now why those moments had seemed so precious. Each had afforded me a glimpse down a tunnel into the past, reminding me that we—mankind, the sudden, savage spoiler, the holder of the spear—are here only because of what preceded us.

Sea turtles and sharks, frigate birds and flamingos—to all of them we owe the respect, the care and the reverence due distinguished ancestors. And perhaps the only ground where we can properly express, or experience, that devotion is in those places where upstart man shrinks to proportion, those places that by some irony of language we call wild.

The Watery Wilds

PHOTOGRAPHS BY JOHN DOMINIS

"Water is the essence of the island," says photographer John Dominis about Dominica, the wettest link in the Antilles chain. And indeed on this remote, most untouched of Caribbean islands, water is everywhere. Endlessly cycled from earth to sky and then back again, it manifests itself in clouds and mists, cataracts and rivers, sea and rain—and in the lush tropical growth. Photographing the island's pervasive water, and the play of light upon it, became Dominis' challenging goal.

John Dominis is no stranger to Dominica. The untamed, sometimes treacherous beauty of the island first enthralled him in 1965, when he journeyed there on an assignment for LIFE. And although his global travels on other photographic assignments have taken him to many of the world's choicest wild places, Dominica has drawn him back on two occasions. "Dominica is my favorite island," he explains, "because it's so stormy and wild."

To take the pictures for this portfolio, Dominis roved the island for two weeks, threading through the dense undergrowth in the high, green interior and picking his way around the island's fringes from the sunwashed Caribbean shore (right) to the rocky eastern coast. Dominica's incessant rainfall drenched him so often that he took to using an underwater camera, even on land. Caught in a short-lived but pelting downpour near the Layou River, he used the submersible equipment to record the seemingly solid wall of rain on page 173.

Of all places on the island, Dominis found himself most attracted to the tempestuous northeast coast on the rugged windward side. There, at a spot called Sandwich Bay, giant waves play a violent drama on the exposed volcanic rocks (page 176) that form the core of this seabound land mass. The rough waters pose a danger for the few swimmers who brave them. And by their relentless pounding, the breakers slowly pulverize the dark rocks into carbonblack sand, from which, in slants of sun, an array of glistening highlights appears with each receding wave.

For the photographer, this lofty, battered tip of Dominica, where the sun always sets behind a screen of clouds, best evoked the island's dramatic nature. And as Dominis flew over it for a last aerial look with his camera, he caught the misty rays of sunset (pages 178-179) emblazoning Dominica's solitary majesty.

A SUNSET FILTERED THROUGH PALM FRONDS

STORM-BLASTED PALMS ON DOMINICA'S WINDWARD COAST

RAINBOW AT LATE AFTERNOON

WILD TAMARIND

FOAMING CATARACT AT TRAFALGAR FALLS

CLOUDBURST OVER THE LAYOU RIVER

HIGH NOON IN THE RAIN FOREST

SURF BREAKING AT SANDWICH BAY

GALAXIES OF LIGHT IN VOLCANIC SAND

SUNSET ON THE NORTH COAST

Bibliography

*Also available in paperback.
†Available only in paperback.

†Abbott, R. Tucker, *How to Know the American Marine Shells*. The New American Library of World Literature, 1961.

Abrahams, Peter, *Jamaica*. Her Majesty's Stationery, London, 1957.

*Arnold, Augusta Foote, *The Sea Beach at Ebb-Tide*. Dover Publications, 1968.

Beard, J. S., *The Natural Vegetation of the Windward and Leeward Islands*. Oxford at the Clarendon Press, 1949.

Blair, Thomas A., and R. Fite, *Weather Elements*. Prentice-Hall, 1963.

Bond, James, *Birds of the West Indies*. Houghton Mifflin Company, 1971.

Britton, N. L., and J. N. Rose, *The Cactaceae,* 2 volumes. Dover Publications, 1963.

Bullard, Fred M., *Volcanoes*. University of Texas Press, 1962.

Burns, Sir Alan, *History of the British West Indies*. George Allen & Unwin, 1954.

Bustard, Robert, *Sea Turtles*. Taplinger Publishing Company, 1972.

Carr, Archie, *So Excellent a Fishe*. Natural History Press, 1967.

Cracknell, Basil E., *Dominica*. Stackpole Books, 1973.

Cromie, William J., *The Living World of the Sea*. Prentice-Hall, 1966.

Fermor, Patrick Leigh, *The Traveller's Tree*. Harper and Brothers, 1950.

Fodor, Eugene, *Guide to the Caribbean*. David McKay Company, 1963.

Fricke, Hans W., *The Coral Seas*. G. P. Putnam's Sons, 1973.

†Greenberg, Jerry and Idaz, *The Living Reef*. Seahawk Press, 1972.

Halstead, Bruce W., M. D., *Dangerous Marine Animals*. Cornell Maritime Press, 1959.

†Hannau, Hans W., and Jeanne Garrard, *Flowers of the Caribbean*. Argos Inc., 1974.

*Hargreaves, Dorothy and Bob, *Tropical Trees*. Hargreaves Industrial, Portland, Oregon, 1965.

Hearn, Lafcadio, *Two Years in the French West Indies*. Gregg Press, 1970.

Heilprin, Angelo, *Mont Pelée and the Tragedy of Martinique*. J. B. Lippincott Company, 1903.

Kennan, George, *The Tragedy of Pelée*. The Outlook Company, 1902.

Kingsbury, John M., *Poisonous Plants of the United States and Canada*. Prentice-Hall, 1964.

Labat, J. B., *The Memoirs of Père Labat*. trans. John Eaden. Frank Cass, 1970.

Lane, Frank W., *The Elements Rage*. David & Charles, 1966.

Little, Elbert L., Jr., and Frank H. Wadsworth, *Common Trees of Puerto Rico and the Virgin Islands*. U. S. Government Printing Office, 1964.

Mitchell, Carleton, *Islands to Windward*. D. Van Nostrand Company, 1948.

Morison, Samuel Eliot, *Admiral of the Ocean Sea*. Little, Brown and Company, 1942.

Murphy, Robert Cushman, *Oceanic Birds of South America,* 2 volumes. Published for The American Museum of Natural History by The Macmillan Company, 1936.

Nichols, David, and John A. L. Cooke, *The Oxford Book of Invertebrates*. Oxford University Press, 1971.

Palmer, Ralph S., ed., *Handbook of North American Birds*. Yale University Press, 1962.

Putnam, William G., *Geology*. Oxford University Press, 1971.

Randall, John E., *Caribbean Reef Fishes*. THF Publications, Hong Kong, 1968.

Ray, Carleton, and Elgin Ciampi, *The Underwater Guide to Marine Life*. A. S. Barnes and Company, 1956.

Rickett, Harold William, *Wild Flowers of the United States,* Volume 4: The Southwestern States. McGraw-Hill Book Company, 1970.

Roberts, W. Adolphe, *Jamaica*. Coward-McCann, 1955.

Robinson, Carey, *The Fighting Maroons of Jamaica*. William Collins and Sangster, Jamaica, 1969.

*Sauer, Carl Ortwin, *The Early Spanish Main*. University of California Press, 1966.

Schauensee, Rodolphe Meyer de, *Guide to the Birds of South America*. Livingston Publishing Company, Wynnewood, Pennsylvania, 1970.

Smith, F. G. Walton, *Atlantic Reef Corals*. University of Miami Press, 1972.

Stephens, William M., *Southern Seashores: A World of Animals and Plants*. Holiday House, 1968.

Vogel, Zdenek, *Reptiles and Amphibians*. The Viking Press, 1964.

Waugh, Alec, *A Family of Islands*. Doubleday and Company, 1964.

Westermann, J. H., and J. I. S. Zonneveld, *Photo-Geological Observations and Land Capability and Land Use Survey of the Island of Bonaire*. Royal Tropical Institute, Amsterdam, 1956.

Wyckoff, Jerome, *Rock, Time and Landforms*. Harper and Row, 1966.

Periodicals and Papers

Diamond, A. W., "Notes on the Breeding Biology and Behavior of the Caribbean Frigate Bird." Unpublished paper.

Doerr, Arthur H., and Don R. Hoy, "Karst Landscapes of Cuba, Puerto Rico and Jamaica." *The Scientific Monthly,* October 1957.

Nelson, Bryan, "The Man-o'-War Bird." *Natural History,* May 1966.

Robinson, E., and J. F. Lewis, *Field Guide to Aspects of the Geology of Jamaica*. University of the West Indies, Mona, Jamaica, no date.

Zans, V. A., L. J. Chubb, H. R. Versey, J. B. Williams, E. Robinson and D. L. Cooke, *Synopsis of the Geology of Jamaica, 1962*. Bulletin No. 4, Geological Survey Department, Jamaica.

Acknowledgments

The author and editors of this book are particularly indebted to Edward Towle, President, Island Resources Foundation, St. Thomas, Virgin Islands. They also wish to thank the following. In Antigua: George Massiah, Minister of Education, St. John's; Barney Thompson, Director of Public Works, St. John's. In Barbuda: The Honorable Victor Browne, Warden of the Island of Barbuda, Codrington. In Dominica: R. B. Blatcher; Peter and Margery Brand; Clarence A. Butler, Chairman, Dominica Tourist Board; Claudette Cools-Lartigue, Executive Secretary, Dominica Tourist Board; Bernard John-Baptiste; Christopher Maximen, Chief Forestry Officer, Botanical Garden. In the Dominican Republic: Alain Liogier, Director of Botany, Jardín Botánico, Santo Domingo. In Grenada: Captain Michael Tate. In Jamaica: Alan Fincham, Department of Biochemistry, University of the West Indies; Hugh Gentles and Arthur Kitchen, Jamaica Tourist Board; Sonya Hamilton, Air Jamaica; William T. Horsfield, Edward Robinson and John Roobol, Department of Geology, University of the West Indies; Bernard Lewis, former Director, Institute of Jamaica; Anthony Porter; Frank and June Gay Pringle. In the Netherlands Antilles: Frater Arnoldo-Broeders, Curaçao; Hugo Gerharts, Bonaire; L. D. Gerharts, Bonaire; Ingvar Kristensen, Director, Caribbean Marine Biological Institute, Curaçao; Don Stewart, Bonaire. In New York City: John L. Behler, Assistant Curator of Herpetology, New York Zoological Society; Dorothy E. Bliss, Department of Fossil and Living Invertebrates, The American Museum of Natural History; Gerald Groves, Consul General of Jamaica; Sidney Horenstein, Department of Fossil and Living Invertebrates, The American Museum of Natural History; Marcella Martinez, Jamaica Tourist Board; Larry G. Pardue, Plant Information Specialist, New York Botanical Garden; Diane Schwartz, Head Reference Librarian, New York Botanical Garden Library; C. Lavett Smith, Department of Ichthyology, The American Museum of Natural History. In the Virgin Islands: Dennis Huffman, Management Assistant, Virgin Islands National Park, St. John; John McEachern, Island Resources Foundation, St. Thomas; William Webb, Superintendent, Virgin Islands National Park, St. John. Also: Ruth Adams, Washington, D.C.; James Bond, Academy of Natural Science, Philadelphia; Anthony W. Diamond, International Council for Bird Preservation, Seychelles; Myron Hokin, President, Century America Corporation, Chicago; Richard Howard, Director, Arnold Arboretum, Jamaica Plain, Massachusetts; Dan Nicholson, Associate Curator of Botany, Smithsonian Institution, Washington, D.C.; Mary Lou Pressick and William Rainey, Department of Zoology, University of California, Berkeley; Paul Tzimoulis, Editor, *Skin Diver's Magazine,* Los Angeles; John Wells, Department of Geological Sciences, Cornell University, Ithaca, New York.

Picture Credits

Index

*Numerals in italics indicate a
photograph or drawing of the subject
mentioned.*

Printed in U.S.A. **X**